Hegel

Phenomenology and System

H. S. HARRIS

Hegel

Phenomenology and System

Hackett Publishing Company, Inc.
Indianapolis/Cambridge

For further information, please address

Hackett Publishing Company, Inc.
P.O. Box 44937
Indianapolis, Indiana 46244-0937

Cover and text design by Dan Kirklin

Library of Congress Cataloging-in-Publication Data

Harris, H. S. (Henry Silton), 1926–
    Hegel: phenomenology and system/H. S. Harris.
       p.   cm.
    Includes bibliographical references and index.
    ISBN 0-87220-282-8 (cloth)   ISBN 0-87220-281-X (pbk.)
    1. Hegel, Georg Wilhelm Friedrich, 1770–1831.
Phänomenologie des Geistes.   I. Title.
B2929.H34 1995
193—dc20   95–32420
                                    CIP

The paper used in this publication meets the minimum requirements of American National Standard for Information Sciences—Permanence of Paper for Printed Library Materials, ANSI Z39.48-1984.

Contents

Preface

This little book is intended for the beginning student of Hegel's *Phenomenology of Spirit*. It aims to provide a skeleton key for the difficult argument of that much larger work. I have written as simply as possible and have sought to *explicate* Hegel's technical vocabulary without using it myself. In order to concentrate on the argument of Hegel's book, I have been compelled to assume that the reader has some knowledge of the history of philosophy from Descartes to Kant—and especially some slight acquaintance with the latter. Apart from providing a skeleton key to the argument— and eliminating some red herrings in the process—I wanted to do two things: to place the *Phenomenology* in the context of Hegel's system as a whole and to show what the aim of the "system" is, in its relation to Kant, Fichte, and Schelling. I have tried to take as little as possible for granted, but if the reader finds the perspective novel—and hence hard to correlate with the historical views that she already has—I can only recommend the policy that is appropriate for the crucial turning point in the argument of the book. One cannot make the argument at the beginning of Hegel's fifth chapter easily intelligible at the first reading; one can only ask the reader to press on and see if things have become clearer when she has grasped the whole story.

Those who are already acquainted with Hegel in some measure may find that the perspective here is novel, because the *Phenomenology* is regarded as the proper key to the system as a whole. Hegel tended, during the years of his great authority at Berlin, to present his system as a rational *theology*. The *Phenomenology* is quite explicitly a philosophical "science of experience," and in experience it is not "God" who is the "measure." What is measured is just what *we* can mean by "God," and it is that "measured" concept that becomes the foundation stone for the "speculative system."

So we must begin "philosophical science" with a careful examination of the sense in which a "science of experience" is possible, and the logical movement of Hegel's book must be brought out. The *Phenomenology* and Hegel's encyclopedic system turn out to be the two sides of the "comprehension of time" as a logical concept.

Hegel's claim that the *Phenomenology* is both the "introduction" to systematic philosophy and its "first part" must be taken with full seriousness. The *Phenomenology* should be thought of as the *logical* theory of finite experience. In its "introductory" aspect, it has the task of overcoming the temporal "standpoint of consciousness" and replacing it with the eternal standpoint of speculative logic, while in its systematic aspect, it is a "science of experience" that provides the comprehensive understanding of historical time. (Comprehensive is an ordinary word that is also a Hegelian technical term.) By grasping the meaning of "logical science," the reader will move from one sense to the other.

The *Phenomenology* is the "first part" of philosophy, conceived as having two parts: the theory of *appearance* (coordinate with the theory of real being) and that of finite cognition (coordinate with speculative cognition). But this means that it is also the "first part" of speculative logic (the "science of experience," coordinate with the "science of logic"), and as the logic of finite cognition it is systematically the first of *three* parts: consciousness, speculative logic, real philosophy.

After the *Phenomenology* was completed, Hegel spent nearly ten years on the elaboration of his *Science of Logic* (the second part). After that, he concentrated for another ten years on the "encyclopedic" presentation of real being (the second part condensed, together with the third). He replaced the *Phenomenology* (in its introductory aspect) with a logical account of the history of modern philosophy. But the *Phenomenology* always continued to be essential to Hegel's system as a whole. It closes the circle of the system as a theory of *human* experience and cognition. The *Philosophy of Spirit* (which ends with the "history of philosophy") cannot return properly to the *Logic* without it. For those who do not accept the radical sublation of religious experience in philosophical speculation, the *Phenomenology* will have only its introductory function. But if the logical circle is understood as it is in this book, we can see in what sense Hegel regarded his philosophy as the *completion* of the task of philosophy. The *Phenomenology* is the conceptual comprehension of *time*, and systematic philosophy generally is the exhibition of the "true infinite" circularity of the temporal and eternal standpoints.

In the perspective of the *Encyclopedia*, the *Phenomenology* becomes the first of *four* parts. We have to recognize the division of "Real Philosophy" into "Philosophy of Nature" and "Philosophy of Spirit" because of the enormous importance that Hegel attaches to the "three syllogisms" of Logic, Nature, and Spirit. But that topic—in which the reconciliation of the theological perspective of Hegel's system with the human-logical one offered here may perhaps be found—must be left to the more advanced student. The unified perspective offered in this book should not be regarded (by the beginners for whom it is intended) as final. But in this new day in which the theory of evolution has turned Nature and Spirit into a conceptual continuum, and the advance of technology has made the evident circularity of "real philosophy" into a burning practical problem, the relevance of the Hegelian system as a tripartite "circle of experience" will be evident enough.

The enormous labor that produced *Hegel's Ladder* laid the foundation for this bird's-eye view of the *Phenomenology* as part of the "system." In that greater endeavor many helped who cannot now be remembered. But I can record here my thanks to the Killam Foundation, which made it possible, by the granting of a Fellowship, for me to write this little book (as well as finish the big one); to my daughter Carol, who typed it onto its disk; to David and Jane, who helped with the index (and in so many other ways); and to Jim Devin and Dan McIntosh (who also helped in many ways and who can serve as the representatives of the many who remain anonymous). The book itself is dedicated to Jim Devin (who has always thought that it was needed, and who thinks still that it could be simpler).

H. S. Harris
May Day, 1995

Abbreviations

W. and C. = G. W. F. Hegel: *Phänomenologie des Geistes*, ed. H.-F. Wessels and H. Clairmont, Hamburg, F. Meiner, 1988.

Miller = G. W. F. Hegel: *Phenomenology of Spirit*, trans. A. V. Miller, Oxford, Clarendon Press, 1977. (References are by *paragraph* number.)

Enz. = *Enzyklopädie der philosophischen Wissenschaften*, (1830) (see *Werke*, Band 8, and *The Encyclopedia Logic*).

Briefe = *Briefe von und an Hegel*, 4 vols, ed. J. Hoffmeister and R. Flechsig, Hamburg, F. Meiner, 1961.

Nicolin = *Hegel in Berichten seiner Zeitgenossen*, ed. G. Nicolin, Hamburg, F. Meiner, 1970.

Chapter 1
System and Experience

1. Philosophical Interests

Aristotle claimed that philosophy begins in wonder. He was certainly correct, but the claim is not definitive. What begins in wonder (before philosophy emerges) is mythmaking about the origin of the world and the creatures in it, especially ourselves. Philosophy was a new kind of storytelling about these topics. The myths were already there, and the first philosophers (at least in the Western tradition) took over some of their assumptions but modified their form. Because of their *cosmological* concern, those first philosophers were "systematic"; they began from a concept of "the whole" and tried to develop it consistently in connection with their fragmentary observations of some parts.

But *practical* philosophical reflection about how we ought to live in the world began at least as early as this cosmological theorizing did; and it was less "systematic" because it was concerned with our limited human capacities and expectations. Some conception of the world as a whole was needed for ethical reflection, but a mythical one would do perfectly well as the frame for the theory of action.

Critical philosophy may well have begun directly from the myths too; for a critical impulse was certainly involved in the emergence of cosmological speculation and perhaps also (quite often) in ethical arguments. But the critical intellect soon found its proper place in the philosophical spectrum as the awareness of the great gap between the theory of the whole and the actual experience of the parts, and as the comparative consciousness of the many discordant ethical views, all unable to defeat or convert one another.

Out of the operation of the critical intellect grew another kind of constructive philosophical reflection, which we can conveniently call *empirical*. The empirical philosophers work in a piecemeal

1

way, not troubling about the concept of the "whole," but accepting some established context of assumptions and seeking to resolve specific conceptual problems or difficulties that have arisen within that context.

We can plausibly divide the empirical type of philosophy into *scientific* philosophy and the philosophy of *common sense*. Scientific philosophy aims at the logical organization and methodical increase of the theoretical knowledge that we derive from our fragmentary experience of the world. It takes us back to the original cosmological impulse, because it must consciously adopt some concept of the world as a whole. But quite opposite assumptions are possible. The commonsense approach makes no assumptions absolutely, but simply accepts the conceptual context that seems "natural" for the problem that is to be resolved (which may be either a matter of the practical conduct of life or a theoretical question).

It is important to realize that all of these traditions of philosophical inquiry remain essentially untouched by Hegel's claim to have defined and solved the "absolute" problem of our philosophical tradition. His theory of "absolute knowing" is a conception of what philosophical knowledge is. The inquiry proceeds at a higher logical level than these first-order (or, in the case of critical philosophy, second-order) types of philosophy. It puts all of them in their logical places in its own more general perspective, and it subjects all of them to fairly radical criticism in order to establish the need for that logically higher perspective. But the criticism does not invalidate any of them; on the contrary, it justifies and validates them. After it is finished, all of them are free to proceed much as before. If they take the logical critique and clarification to heart, they will be better able not to get in one another's way, and will be saved from much useless and wasteful polemic. But the dawn of "absolute knowing" does not inhibit the pursuit of finite knowledge in any of its forms, either empirical or philosophical.

2. Hegel's Philosophical Problem

An "original" thinker does not choose her philosophy; it grows upon her out of the problems that arise spontaneously in her life. No problem, and no solution, can possibly change (or seriously affect) the range of serious concerns that may preoccupy other thinkers. All of the varieties of philosophy that I have enumerated were in full flower when Hegel was in school, and they all continue to flourish. He was relatively peculiar, because he wanted to put them all in their places in his own "System." He was a new kind of "systematic" philosopher, because he was concerned not so much about the world as about the varieties of our experience of it. His "absolute knowledge" is the clear understanding of what human knowing is. The solution of this problem—if we suppose that he has solved it—does not affect anything else that we may want to know about the world; at the most it will provide us with a new perspective upon our curiosity.

Hegel thought, of course, that his problem *was* the "absolute" problem of philosophy—the one that philosophers had been struggling with, more or less consciously, from the first. He received his higher education in a theological seminary, after receiving classical training in earlier years. So he knew all about the pre-Christian myths; and the Christian Bible became for him the mythology of his own community, which had to be turned into philosophy. Our knowledge of "God" was the one "absolute" problem of philosophy.

It was through Kant that this theological problem became the problem of human knowledge in general. Kant had succeeded in establishing the "critical" perspective as the arbiter of what was possible in all kinds of philosophical inquiry. In this view, we must accept our finite status as an absolute limit upon our theoretical knowledge. The highest philosophical knowledge we can achieve is the understanding of the categories through which we structure our fragmentary experience into the world that we all share. We have *no* knowledge of whether or not "God exists" (the current alternative assumptions for "scientific" philosophy at that time). We can afford to suspend judgement about this, because the unity of our world arises from the structure and operation of our experiencing minds.

In our relations with one another, however, we do have some "absolute" knowledge of how we must behave (or so Kant thought); and therefore we are entitled to make some *postulates* about God's existence and our relations with him. To Hegel, this compromise, in which "rational faith" took the place of the "absolute knowledge" that is theoretically impossible, gradually became unacceptable. He accepted from Kant the "critical" view that we must begin by investigating what we actually know and how and why we know it. But this had the effect of directing his attention in an open-minded and critical way to the question of how "God" enters our world as an actual object of *experience*. What knowledge of the absolute being is and what can be known "absolutely" became *critical* questions for Hegel. Kant had argued that the disagreements of "scientific" philosophers prove that we have no rationally intuitive knowledge of ultimate reality; but in that case why should we assume that we have an intuitive understanding of what knowledge is at all? We ought to consider what has been taken to be "knowledge" in an unprejudiced manner.

This approach leads to a closer examination of how and why our "categorical" knowledge gets its *objective* status. We are not born with the minds of scientific observers already in full working order. So how do we come to have them, and why should the world that they constitute for us be privileged as a "reality" as opposed to the world of our tribal storytellers?

Initially, Hegel did not have this problem of the justification of *scientific* knowledge. He was concerned only about the quality of the popular *faith*. Kant and Fichte produced their versions of the rational faith just as Hegel was completing his studies in orthodox Lutheran theology. But by then, he was convinced that the *political* faith of the Hellenes was the paradigm for the "living religion" that his own age needed. Somehow the quality of the Greek experience had to be restored within the universal conceptual system of the Kantian philosophy. It was only after he had spent several years working out a solution to this problem (in a manuscript that is now almost entirely lost) that Hegel moved on to the problem of resolving "faith" into "knowledge."

It was Schelling who produced the initial solution for the "faith and knowledge" problem (though, as we shall see in the next chapter, Hölderlin was more important in the development of Hegel's own thought). At Jena, Hegel became the official "logician" for the new speculative idealism in which the "Identity" theory was stated. The speculative identity of Thought and Being is a Spinozist identity of God and Nature which is known to a thought that is consciously *free* (in the Kantian practical sense). But Hegel was always dissatisfied with Schelling's appeal to "intellectual intuition" as the foundation for this speculative knowledge. The position of philosophical common sense is just as intuitive as any critical or speculative standpoint can ever be. Thus, in the end, the problem of providing the philosophically disposed "natural consciousness" with a "ladder to the Absolute" emerged. That is the problem of the *Phenomenology* (in its character as the "introduction to speculative philosophy"). But the solution turns out to be also the establishment of a new philosophical science on its own account: the "science of the experience of consciousness." This "Science" replaces the *critically* scientific philosophy of Kant; it shows that if we regard our experience of the community as the *substantial* foundation of our own rational selfhood, and our experience of God as the community's experience of its own substantial subjectivity, there is no need for the postulational extension of Reason into "rational faith" at all.

This continuity of Reason with Faith is attractive to the religious consciousness, because "God" is experienced in religion as the real mover of the process of salvation for the singular consciousness and its finite community. There are some strong indications in Hegel's *Philosophy of World History* that he was willing to countenance a "speculative faith." He not only presents world history as the movement of "Providence" (as if a superhuman agent were really involved), but also employs the myth of a "March of the Spirit" from the Sunrise towards the Sunset to support a "substantial" interpretation of the great Asian cultures as logically primitive.

Every aspect of this concept of history as the work of a *real* "Divine Providence" is superstitious and reactionary. What we now know about the cultural movement of religious ideas (and especially about the spread of Buddhism) shows that the March of the Spirit is an unhistorical fiction; and Hegel's interpretation of non-Christian cultures shows clear signs of the nascent cultural and economic imperialism of Western Europe in his time (and in the ensuing century).

Hence, the position adopted here is that we should interpret Hegel's philosophy strictly as a Science and ignore all of the "religious" extensions of it made by Hegel or others. In this perspective, the "Science of experience," being the speculatively integrated version of Kant's Critical Philosophy, provides the true criterion of what is genuinely scientific in Hegel. The *Philosophy of World History* shows us the weak side of Hegel's philosophy—it is "speculative" in the bad sense. The *Phenomenology* is the book that contains Hegel's genuine theory of historical knowledge. Our present object is to discover in it the interpretation of Hegel's system that remains "eternally" valid.

Chapter 2
Hegel's Life and Works

1. Stuttgart and Tübingen

Georg Wilhelm Friedrich Hegel (*Wilhelm* in his family life) was born in Stuttgart on 27 August 1770; in later years he liked to prolong his birthday celebrations after midnight, so as to share them with Goethe, who was just twenty-one years older than he. Our philosopher was the first child of Georg Ludwig Hegel, a senior civil servant in the Duchy of Württemberg; in the course of a few years he acquired a sister, Christiane, who was always deeply attached to him, and a brother, Karl. Their mother, Maria Magdalena (Fromm), taught Wilhelm his letters and was much concerned about his early education. She died when he was only thirteen, but it is plausible to think that she did much to set his feet early on the path towards an academic career.

In school Hegel excelled. At the Stuttgart Gymnasium, he received a solid grounding in classical languages and literature. When he went on to the Theological Seminary at Tübingen (in 1788), he probably knew already that he wanted to be a teacher, rather than a Lutheran pastor. He was firmly opposed to the theological fundamentalism of G. C. Storr, who sought to put his own belief in the Saviour (securely certified as the true Son of God by the miraculous context and content of his life) into the "room" that the Kantian critical philosophy had made for "faith."

At Tübingen Hegel met Hölderlin, who was just five months older than himself and already dedicated to a poetic vocation. They were drawn together by their shared love for Hellenic civilization, and especially for Plato and Sophocles. Hegel was already a voracious reader of modern philosophical and social studies; he read Kant, but was better known among his friends as a constant student of Rousseau and Lessing. In 1790, Schelling arrived in the Seminary; a recognized intellectual prodigy, he was at the head of his class at age fifteen. Across the Rhine, the Revolution was in full

flower, and many students were more interested in what was happening there than they were in their official studies. Those who
sympathized with the Revolution formed a political club, and
Hegel—who was never much of an orator, on the academic side,
either then or later—is said to have been a "flaming sword" in his
political speeches (*Briefe* I, pp. 394–395, 2 Feb. 1812). Schelling was
soon on the carpet before the Duke, charged with the heinous of-
fence of translating the "Marseillaise."

In his last year at the Seminary, Hegel wrote his first "philosophical" essay. He discusses the great gulf between the essentially political religion of the Greek cities and the private religion
of his own Lutheran community in Württemberg; he also draws a
sharp distinction between dead "objective" theology and living
"subjective" religious experience. We can see that he has read
Kant's *Religion* and Fichte's *Critique of All Revelation*, but his enterprise is inspired by a hope (which he owes to Rousseau, and probably also to Lessing and Herder) that something like the civil
religion of the ancients can be revived. When the essay breaks off
in the middle of an attack on the "modern spirit," we can recognize (I think) the closest and most powerful influence of all—that
of Hölderlin. The dreamy nostalgia of the poet bewitched Hegel,
but his own sturdy realism pulled him up short here. We must be
thinking of what is now possible, not of what is lost beyond actual
recall.

2. Berne and Frankfurt

When Hegel left the Seminary, he obtained a post as house-tutor
in the aristocratic family of the von Steigers in Switzerland. He
went off to Berne for three years, where his duties left him plenty
of time for his own studies and writing. He was lonely and rather
unhappy, but also indefatigably productive. After some wrestling
with the problem that defeated him in his Tübingen essay, he began to find his way forward. He wrote first a "Life of Jesus" from
which all the miracle stories that Storr depended upon are excluded. The miracles of healing are interpreted as poetic meta-
phors for the power of psychological conversion (healing the
blindness of prejudice and the deafness of convention, breaking
the fetters of tradition), and the rest are silently eliminated. Then
came an essay which sought to explain how the teaching of this

saint of Reason degenerated into a "positive" faith in the Gospel that he brought to us from God. Jesus had to operate in the thought-context of his society. If he was to teach at all, he could not help becoming "the Master"; and soon he was "the Messiah." He could not help being opposed to the authoritarian structure of his society, so the Reformers who tried to return to his teaching could not help creating a religion of the inner life, realized through the endless multiplication of separate sects in the outer world.

Hegel was still working on this "Positivity" essay in 1796 when he heard, through Hölderlin, of a teaching post in a great merchant family in Frankfurt. Hölderlin himself was a house-tutor in Frankfurt, so the two friends were joyfully reunited there at the beginning of 1797. Hegel's studies, which had already turned back towards the "Hellenic Ideal" of the Tübingen essay, took on a powerful Romantic tinge as soon as the prospect of a move to Frankfurt dawned. His concept of "Spirit" was born at Frankfurt, though it was not more than half conceptualized while he was there. The context of all his joint speculation with Hölderlin was the theological doctrine "In God we live, and move, and have our being." The Greeks, they agreed, had achieved the true consciousness of this "union," but the relationship between the Infinite Life (of God or "Nature") and the finite life of human communities can be immensely various. This relationship is the "spirit" of the community. Hegel (who was reading Thucydides as he pondered why "Christianity conquered paganism") ought perhaps to have been more sceptical about the perfection of the "Hellenic Ideal" than he seems to have been. But as he studied the Old Testament and developed his account of the degeneration of Abraham's religion into the "positive divine law" of Moses, he also constructed a theory of the "forms of Union" in the loss and recovery of unity with God. Every "spirit" generates its own "fate" (the side of the Infinite Life that it alienates from itself). That is why the story that we read in Thucydides has ominous implications for the Hellenic Ideal. But Jesus now personifies the absolute Spirit of "reconciliation with fate." His gospel of God's love is the summons to a new life that rises above the spirit of Kantian morality, just as it rises above the natural happiness of Abraham and the positive obedience of Moses. Kantian morality, in fact, is just the internalized shape of Mosaic obedience. How much the presence of Hölderlin contributed to this vision we cannot precisely say. But there are solid grounds for claiming that the manuscript we call "The Spirit of Christianity and Its Fate" was the most passionately *beautiful* piece that Hegel ever wrote.

Hegel revised his manuscript about a year after he drafted it (i.e., in 1800), and in the revision he discovered the conceptual process of *Aufhebung*. To begin with, this word, which he borrowed from Schiller, had designated the complete cancelling (or drowning) of the lower relation in the higher; the ideal of moral righteousness is completely *forgotten* in the experience of God's love. But in the revision, *Aufhebung* came to have its *preservative* aspect. The gospel of Jesus *fulfils* the law of Moses, and the law becomes a stage on the way to that "fulfilment" which must not be altogether forgotten, because it retains a certain (heavily qualified) validity.

3. Jena and Schelling

Early in 1799 Hegel's father died. By the end of the year, the estate was settled and Hegel had received a modest inheritance. He seems to have been free of his tutorial duties in 1800. He completed a large manuscript (now lost), which he thought of, then, as his "System"; and at the end of the year he wrote to Schelling (already a professor at Jena), asking advice about how he (Hegel) could embark on an academic career. Schelling urged him to come to Jena and begin on the spot. That was surely what he was hoping to hear, so he went at once.

At Jena, he was universally regarded as Schelling's ally and disciple. His first publication was the essay *Difference Between the Systems of Fichte and Schelling*, in which Schelling's philosophy of nature was shown to be a necessary development of the new speculative idealism, and one which Fichte ought not to reject. Hegel obtained his licence to teach with the Latin thesis *On The Orbits of the Planets*, and he promptly began to teach the "Logic and Metaphysics" of the speculative union with God. It gave him much trouble, and he produced several versions of it during his first teaching career. In spite of repeated promises, he did not publish any of them, and only one has survived. The difficult gestation of the *Phenomenology of Spirit* had begun.

In 1802, Hegel began to teach "Natural Law." This was the "caterpillar shape" of his later Philosophy of Spirit, and in its highest reaches the "forms of Union" now became a "biography of God."

Schelling and Hegel were joint editors of the short-lived *Critical Journal of Philosophy*. Everything in it was anonymous, but Hegel wrote most of it, including the long essay *Faith and Knowledge* (springing from his *logical* concerns) and an almost equally long essay on *Natural Law*.

In 1803, when Schelling left Jena, Hegel's "System" took on the "encyclopaedic" pattern that it never lost. He worked furiously to develop his own "philosophy of nature" in order to bind together his "speculative theory" and his "real philosophy." He was beginning to be in desperate financial straits, and he needed a professorship. In spite of his astounding industry, the evolution of his thought was always too fast for him; early in 1805 he abandoned a "fair copy" of his System when it was approximately half written.

That was the point at which the *Phenomenology of Spirit* was born. We shall discuss that project in the next chapter. For the moment, we must complete the bare outline of Hegel's career. He managed to sketch the new *metaphysical* Logic and to rewrite the Real Philosophy (of Nature and Spirit) which this "Science of Experience" was designed to introduce, in his lecture courses, while he was writing the book. The publisher had begun to print it before it had been completed, and Hegel was both using the proof sheets for his Logic lectures and spending the author's honorarium. He had to finish the book in a great hurry, because his friend Niethammer had promised to pay the publisher's costs if Hegel had not furnished the completed manuscript by October of 1806.

4. Bamberg, Heidelberg, Nuremberg, Berlin

The battle of Jena made it impossible for Hegel to send the last installment of the *Phenomenology* by the due date. It was also the last straw for his academic career. He had no money, and his pregnant housekeeper depended upon him for support. So to Bamberg, as editor of the local newspaper, he went in March 1807, one month after the birth of his son Ludwig Fischer. There he remained until December 1808, when he obtained the position of headmaster of the Gymnasium in Nuremberg. There, at the age of forty, he married into the old merchant nobility. For eight years he taught his System to the upper classes of the school while he worked on the *Science of Logic* which was the completion of the *speculative* half of the system. In that great book (first volume, 1812; third and final volume, 1816), the *Phenomenology* is still explicitly presupposed as the necessary introduction. But when he finally received the call to a professorship at Heidelberg, he profited from the years of pedagogical simplification and produced a very condensed *Encyclopaedia*, which was self-contained.

Ten years later, at Berlin, he produced a much expanded version of the *Encyclopaedia* that included a sizable "introduction" to the standpoint of his speculative logic through the history of modern philosophy since Descartes and Locke. This was, in effect, the final shape of his "system," for the revisions in the final edition of 1831 were minor. The *Phenomenology of Spirit* seemed in the end to have become superfluous. Yet in the last year of his life, Hegel began to revise the two great works of his Napoleonic years; death took him before he finished working on either of them. With the *Phenomenology* he had barely begun. We can see that he intended to divorce that work completely from the Berlin "system" and present it in a free-standing shape, but clearly he regarded it as valid on its own account. Hegel would not have reissued an old book just because it would sell now that he was famous.

Famous he certainly was in his Berlin years. The world of hope that produced his two great books had passed away by the time the second was completed. Napoleon had fallen, and the Restoration was in full swing when Hegel finally became a professor. He went from Heidelberg to Berlin in 1818. The only new book that he published there (in 1821) was the *Philosophy of Right*; this was a developed outline of his theory of the objective actuality of the Spirit. Shielded as it was by an outwardly "conservative" Preface, it became (and remained) the focus of progressive interpretations, radical criticism, and general controversy. After that, Hegel's best work went into his lecture courses—and especially into the great surveys of the forms of Absolute Spirit: Art, Religion, and Philosophy.

Hegel fell ill and died, fairly suddenly, in November of 1831, in the midst of a cholera epidemic. Whether it was really the cholera that killed him, I do not think we can be sure. He was survived by his (much younger) widow Marie and his two legitimate sons (Ludwig had died a few months earlier in the Dutch East Indies).

Chapter 3
The Project of a "Science of Experience"

1. "God" and "Science"

We have seen that, even at Berlin, when his first big book served no longer either as the "introduction" to or as a recognized "part" of his philosophical system, Hegel still believed that the *Phenomenology of Spirit* could stand on its own as a valid philosophical "whole"—a philosophical science in its own right. The principal task of this present short book will be to investigate what the relation was between the *Phenomenology* and the earlier "system" of which it was said to be both the "introduction" and the "first part." But it will be well to begin at the end and ask what the book contains when it stands by itself, quite independent of the "Encyclopaedia of the Philosophical Sciences."

The answer is not difficult to state. The first subtitle that Hegel gave to his book (before it became *Phenomenology of Spirit*) was "Science of the Experience of Consciousness." In his "Introduction," Hegel states both a very simple and abstract concept of "consciousness" (the subjective cognition of an object that is "other" than the knowing self) and a more complex concept of "experience" (the moving process of cognition that generates a new conceptual object by discovering the incoherence, or "contradiction," of the one that was originally posited). This moving process, he says, will come to a halt when the posited concept is seen to agree perfectly with the object as experienced. Since the "motion" is the logical process of "experience" itself, we can quite properly say that the whole book is about the gradual formation of an adequate concept of what "experience" is. Hegel's *Phenomenology* is the "science of experience."

But it is also plain in the "Introduction" that the goal of our quest is "absolute knowledge"—and that this is equivalent to the true knowledge of what "absolutely" *is*. Hegel clearly implies that "the Absolute" has to be "with us" from the beginning, and that if

13

it were not, we could never reach it at all. Hence, some interpreters—notably Heidegger—have argued that the book is completely devoted to the task of revealing the *presence* of the Absolute. The *presence (parousia)* of the divine spirit "with us" is to be regarded as the necessary presupposition of the whole enterprise.

We cannot say categorically that this reading is *wrong*, for, as we have seen, the theological context of speculative idealism is the doctrine that "in *God* we live, and move, and have our being." So, of course, the speculative idealist is committed to the claim that God is always "present." We are always "in His presence," and any inquiry that has "absolute knowing" as its goal can be viewed and presented as the progressive *uncovering* of this truth. It is easy to show, nevertheless, that this is a misleading and perverse way of interpreting what Hegel is doing. The presence of God (or of the Spirit) is in no intelligible sense a *presupposition* of our inquiry. We do not begin with God, but with the *world*—with "night" and "day," and with our own home-world of "house" and "tree"; and we go on to the commonsensical theory of a universe of finite "things." The most committed theologian would agree that (insofar as it is possible to do so) we are moving *away* from God.

Hegel says, in one of his early letters to Schelling, that he once had the idea of discussing "what it might mean to draw near to God" (*Briefe* I, Letter 14; Butler and Seiler, p. 41). The *Phenomenology* does eventually "draw near to God," so in spite of its winding path through "things" (and eventually "atheism"), we might claim that it does fulfil that tentative plan. But, on the one hand, those who are still "far" from God are "living and moving" in Him as much as are those who are "near"; and, on the other hand, our journey does not stop when we achieve the true consciousness of God. We go on beyond that point. The final object of our knowledge is not "God," but ourselves as *knowers*. Ours is not a "journey of the mind to God," but a transformation of philosophy (the *love* of wisdom) into the logical science of our own being in the world.

2. Critical Logic and "Metaphysics"

Kant taught everyone who understood him why there could be no human knowledge of what absolutely *is* "in itself." Our experience is the empirical cognition of a world of finite sensible things, and in order to "know" anything we must *categorize* what the

senses give us; all of our effective knowledge arises from this "syn-
thesis" of the empirical and the intellectual components. We do
not "know" any purely intellectual things—such as God or the
angels in the older theological tradition. We do not, and cannot,
even know *ourselves* as the intellectual "thinking Substances" that
Descartes took us to be. We can only know our feelings and desires
empirically, just as we know our bodies and the world-order of
space and time in which they exist.

We can, however, think through our finite situation in "consciousness" consistently; we can decide what the boundaries of
our cognitive experience are, because we can clearly distinguish
between what is empirical in our consciousness and what is logical (or "necessary"). It was this "logical" knowledge that interested Kant's "speculative" successors. Its existence implies that
there are some purely "intellectual things" that we *do* know, after
all—not God and his angels, or our own "souls," but the structure
of concepts through which we construct, out of the "manifold" of
sensation, the one world of our commonsense existence and our
empirical science. Thus, we do not know that we are ourselves
"thinking substances," but we do know that we are "thinking activities"; and Kant himself held that wherever we could recognize
another "thinking activity," it was our *categorical* obligation to behave towards it with a certain kind of *absolute* respect. Fichte
thought that the endless pursuit and organization of the finite
knowledge that can never establish its own absolute truth could
find here its logically necessary *absolute* foundation or presupposition. Through the requirement of absolute respect for the thinking
agent, he returned, in effect, to the Cartesian world in which finite
thinkers know themselves to be real *substances* ("immortal souls")
living and moving "in God."

But this will not do. Ordinary common sense has never paid
any attention to "metaphysical" theories of this sort. One may be
"religious" in this sense or one may not, but if one is not, philosophical reasoning will not make one so. Kant showed us why we
must not expect that it ever will have that power, and that is one
reason why his theory is so persuasive. Common sense can go on
building our understanding of the world piecemeal, without wor-
rying about whether we "absolutely" understand anything. There
is something problematic about the *categorical* obligation of our
Reason in any case. People *do* tell lies with benevolent motives,

while some who are scrupulously honest and respectful of others' rights seem not to care much about anyone but themselves (and their self-image).

Hegel's early essays in "logic and metaphysics" were dominated by an ideal of *theoretical* continuity. Kant's theory of the intellect, as a systematic structure of categories for the interpretation of our finite experience, was to be put together as a "reflective" image of the *metaphysical* (or *absolute*) standpoint. But even if this could be done, it was obvious that Kant had armed common sense with enough critical weapons to maintain its indifference and its independence. That independence could be shaken only by an altogether different approach to human rationality. Hegel's years with Greek literature and the Bible, with Hölderlin and the "biography of God," taught him that rationality has a *history*. Everyone knows that, in order to be morally rational in the modern way, we must be properly educated. But our education itself is enough to show us that there may already have been forms of rational life that are in some ways preferable to our own. If our religious and philosophical education has somehow brought us to the intuitive conviction not only that all true thinking belongs to a single scientific "system," but also that the same "universal Reason" is present everywhere in the historic experience of human communities (including those "happier" ones), then perhaps the right—the convincing—introduction to speculative wisdom is a developmental account of how rationality has revealed itself in the story of our culture.

The *Phenomenology* is a melding of Hegel's belief that critical logic could be organized into a systematic introduction for the true metaphysics with his concern for the emergence of the "one universal Reason" in history. "Logic and metaphysics" proper have collapsed into "speculative philosophy"; all of it belongs to "pure thinking" and is beyond the level of ordinary empirical consciousness. But the "critical logic" of the earlier years has joined hands with "common sense" by accepting its sensible embodiment. Common sense is to go with us step by step from its own world of houses and trees to the threshold of "pure thinking." It will not be asked to make any acts of faith on rational grounds or to believe anything that it does not spontaneously believe already. Its spontaneous beliefs will be transformed on the way, but in the end they will be restored to it unharmed. What the study of Hegel's book achieves is an enlargement of horizons and (perhaps) of sympathies. We may want to say some things differently after we have read it properly, but we need not do so. We shall certainly have a new perspective on what we believe—a new view of it.

3. The Motion of "Experience"

Our ordinary way of being conscious of the world and gaining knowledge of it—the attitude that Kant analysed—is called by Hegel "the natural consciousness"; and he says that it "will prove itself to be only the concept of knowing, not real knowing" (W. and C. 60:38–39; Miller ¶78). What he means by "the concept of knowing" here is the simple form of subjective awareness of an object that is "other than" the awareness, so that the object is (and continues to be) what it is, whether the subject is aware of it or not. Instead of becoming Kantian sceptics about the "thing-in-itself," we should put our trust in the naive conviction that what appears to us truly *is* in the way that it appears. We shall have a Kantian sceptical experience with this object. We shall discover that our *concept* of knowing is not "real knowing" at all. But if we concentrate not upon the object known, but upon our concept of what it means to know it, we shall find that the concept of knowing evolves in the experience; and instead of becoming "absolute"—as Kant's scepticism does, when the "thing-in-itself" is fully clarified—our scepticism will be "self-completing." In other words, we shall be driven eventually to abandon the standpoint of consciousness altogether—that is the standpoint that generates the "thing-in-itself."

The important thing about our "concept of knowing"—as an object of consciousness—is that it is entirely *within* our consciousness. We do know (or at least we think that we know) what knowing *is* "in itself." We know *what we mean* when we claim to know something. In the ordinary way, we employ this knowledge as the standard by which we decide whether some experience was a *veridical* one. But we can also say that it is the objective content of the experience that "truly is." That is how we "learn by experience"; we form our concept in accordance with our experience of the object. Learning by experience is a matter of accumulating experiences and preserving them in memory. Thus, at first, we shall say that what is *really there* is what we are aware of *right now*—for instance, the Sun setting. But as night passes, the Sun rises, and in due course it sets again; so then we find ourselves saying that what is *always* there is the cycle of day and night (even though it is never there "at this moment.") Then, as the *seasons* pass and return, we realize that it is the cycle of the *year* that is really there; and finally we discover the "Great Year" in the motions of the heavenly bodies. The Sun is the focal point of all this experience, and if we ask "what is *that*, before we ever experience it, and independent of our experience?" we cannot answer. If we concentrate on our experience as what is there *for us*, however, the concept changes but no insoluble problems arise.

We ordinarily assume that *what is there* is the same all the time and that it is only our "concept" of it that changes and develops. But the meaning of "is there" changes with every development of our concept. This change goes on "behind the back of consciousness," as Hegel puts it (W. and C. 68:2; Miller ¶87), because attention is focussed on the unchanging object as it is "in itself." But if we attend to "the second in-itself" (or "what is in itself for us") we can see what is going on, because we are turning around and looking the other way, so to speak. It is the accumulation of our experience that brings about the evolution of our concept of time, until we finally discover "what *eternally* is" in the heavens; and Hegel claims that if we will only turn around and observe the moving concept of our experience, we shall find that it generates a new "shape" whenever our concept of the object passes over from "the first in itself" to the second. The object that is *in itself for us* "contains the nothingness" of what was simply *in itself*.

Using an elementary example makes it easy to see what this means. If I sleep late, then I do not know that the Sun is shining. When I wake up, the fact that the Sun was up although I did not know it is abolished by my knowing that the Sun is high in the sky. The truth has changed, and what was true before has become impossible; and as long as I am dealing with what I do "know" (i.e., with what is *in itself for me*), I can find an appropriate way of determining whether it is *true* or not.

What evolves in the Science of Experience is the standard by which the truth-testing is done. Hegel claims that the standard of what is true is only recognized to have failed because it has cumulatively generated the new standard out of its failure. In part, this knowledge-process is an educational experience that we go through as individuals. We all learn to organize our experience by days, weeks, and years; this happens painlessly through the simple accumulation of our remembered time. Similarly, we move from a world of things with names to a world of things with essential natures, and from there to the "order of Nature" with its laws. These "concepts" are readily available, and we go back and forth between them without strain.

But, in part, the evolution is *historical*. We do not believe now that the human community is *naturally* divided into freemen and slaves, and (at least among the philosophically inclined) few would say, "woman's place is in the home." (In this respect, we have moved on since Hegel's time, when this proposition appeared to be a valid part of the classical heritage. It will be interesting to see how this motion is possible even after the concept of "experience" has become logically complete—as it must have done if Hegel can make a "Science" of it.)

Cognitive *experience* is the progressive discovery of *truth*. In our simpler example of the cumulative experience of *time*, we can see readily how the quest for an adequate concept leads us both to the "eternal" standpoint (which seems to be the *opposite* of time and is logically abstracted as such) and to the great "inversion" that we call "the Copernican Revolution." Hegel's claim is that revolutions and the generation of "opposites" have occurred a number of times in our quest for philosophical *truth* without our being clearly aware of what was happening. Empirically, our experience has been to give up some idea (or just to forget it, and no longer recognize that it was ever there at all) and *find* a new one. The forgetting (or the surrendering) happens *because* we find the new idea; and we are sometimes, but not usually, conscious of that—as in a religious "conversion," or in the "Copernican Revolution" itself. What we are *never* directly conscious of is the fact that it was the cumulative development of the old concept that *led* us to the new one. What appears to be a piece of contingent good fortune, the finding of something new, is actually a logical *result*, the answer to the problem that emerged as critically important in our lives when we were living within the earlier categorical framework.

I have said more than once already that what evolves is our concept of "the truth." But it is not the familiar theoretical concept of "how the *world* truly is" that occupies our attention for the most part. We *begin* with that, because that is where the concept of truth is consciously born. But the evolution of that concept is soon completed. Our main concern is with "philosophy as the guide of life"; we are in quest of the truth about our human goal. The elementary truth that emerges when our concept of "the world" is fully formed is that our intelligence is a *free* activity in it. The discovery of the adequate concept of *rational human freedom* occupies the rest of the book. The whole process is cumulative. Everything that we learn stays with us (or should stay with us). When we learn to think in centuries and to plan our lives in years (or decades), we do not lose the capacity to enjoy the present moment or to live from day to day. But these more finite activities change their significance, and that is also what happens to our concepts.

What happens in life is muddier, more confused, and less conscious than what happens in thought. The "science of experience" is much *clearer* than experience itself is (though it has not seemed so to most students of Hegel's text) precisely because it is *scientific*. This is "our contribution." Our task is to be scientific *observers*, and the philosophical science that we are concerned with is *logic*. Eventually, our motion becomes the progression of human culture in historical time. We shall then be able to say, sometimes, that an interpretation is mistaken because it is historically absurd. But until we reach the level of the "World-Spirit" that is "in time," only our grasp of the cumulative logical development can show us where we go next, and why. Even in the progress of the World-Spirit, it will be logic that guides and controls our interpretive periodization. History does not carry its philosophical significance directly upon its face (as the cycle of the seasons may seem to do, after a few repetitions).

Hegel calls our journey "the way of despair" (W. and C. 61:5; Miller ¶78). Since even the "self-completion of scepticism" happens "behind the back" of consciousness, it is not surprising that *despair* only becomes a direct "experience of consciousness" once (in the Unhappy Consciousness); but *for us* the whole process becomes visible as a "way of the Cross." In the "Introduction," Hegel speaks of the "stations" on our way, but not of the Crucifixion at the end of it. In the last sentence of the book, we do come to "the skull-place of the Absolute Spirit" (i.e., to Calvary or Golgotha). The symbol of our passing beyond the standpoint of "consciousness" altogether is the *death* of God and Man for each other in a shared sacrifice of their status as objects of consciousness. The

Absolute Spirit whose infinity foams forth for it in the resurrection from that death is the goal that is as necessarily fixed as the logical series of stations that will bring us to it. This is where truth as concept and truth as object will correspond perfectly.

We can hardly expect to understand this climax here at the beginning; long before we get to it, we shall have left the ordinary standpoint of the natural consciousness behind. When we reach "Spirit," we shall be observing human communities as "shapes of consciousness," and we shall have to discover how a community can be said to be "conscious." Then (in "Religion") the community faces its God(s) as its own "other self"; and we have to observe these Absolute Spirits—the interaction of the "finite" spirit of the actual community with its "infinite" counterpart—as "shapes of consciousness." How all this can be interpreted without a break in the logical development of the concept of "experience" we must find out as we go. Perhaps, if the logical continuity can be understood and maintained, the final terminus will validate itself *as* final, just as Hegel promises that it will do. For the present, we can only be patiently truthful; and we will begin, as he recommends, by committing ourselves fearlessly to the naive faith that our experience is an actual cognition of what truly is.

Chapter 4
Consciousness

1. Introductory

In the "Table of Contents" that was issued when the last sheets were printed, with a list of *errata* and other such things, Hegel gave the title "Consciousness" to his first three chapters together. In the *Phenomenology* itself, they appear as a simple sequence, with the titles "Sense-Certainty," "Perception," and "Understanding." This sequence (which indicates the phases that our concept of "the world" goes through) continually recurs later as a pattern in the development of self-conscious Reason (i.e., the mode of Self-Consciousness that has recognized its conceptual *identity* with the "world"). We can recognize the three phases readily enough, because they live together side by side in our ordinary consciousness; what we are not normally aware of is the need to arrange them in a progressive sequence. We pick them up and put them down at our convenience, according to the need of the moment.

The first two conceptual schemes are needed by everyone, all the time. The simplest one tells us that we are directly (or *immediately*) aware of "what truly is" through our senses. We *see* the world first as a great moving process in *time*; the movement of time transforms everything, and in the end it carries everything away. But, for a time, we are *here*, and our abiding spatial environment is filled with concrete singular things (*Sachen*) to which we can give *names*.

Most of these names are "common nouns" that can be applied to many concrete things. We make our first step in philosophy when we become interested in how the names stand not for the singular things, but for the *concept* of the thing, the *Ding*. But we need not be conscious of any change in our concept of the world when this happens. We can simply say that we have become interested in how "names" work. Surely this new interest does not change anything that is really there? And although we need "concepts" as well as our "real things" (we must make *plans* to replace what time carries away, for example), we are not obliged to become *philosophically* concerned about our language.

This philosophical interest forces itself upon us only when we begin wanting to *understand* how and why, in spite of the all-devouring stream of time, "the world" somehow stably persists. For now we need to know how the conceptual "essences" of our real things are constituted; and this soon brings us to the "order of Nature." As *scientists*, we return to the problem of time and resolve it in our concept of an eternally stable "substance" (the "Great Year" of the heavenly motions, for example). We ought to be more troubled than we usually are, about the concepts by means of which this substantial concept is formulated, since we cannot regard them as a merely linguistic superstructure piled onto the system of "real things." But we assume, comfortably, that the "laws of Nature" are a non-sensible kind of "being" that is *beyond* or *behind* the "real things" with which we began. Thus, our three conceptual schemes sit side by side in our minds, because they appear to be easily reconciled. But if we meditate on the history of their emergence, we see that this is not so.

2. Sense-Certainty

The story of this emergence has been logically *composed* by the philosophical observer. Our knowledge begins as a sense-consciousness. Sense-experience is infinitely *rich*, both in the sense that we keep on extending its range and in the sense that we can go farther and deeper into something that we have experienced already. But all we can ever *say* at the level of immediate awareness is: "This *is*" and "This is what *I* am aware of." If we focus our attention on some singular instance of sense-knowledge, we realize that this focussing is possible precisely because *this* object (say, the sunset) is *my* object; but the self who is having this experience is also identified precisely by the object. I know *myself* as the one who is seeing this sunset. With the identification that makes experience properly cognitive, *mediation* has already begun.

I chose the sunset because it happens for me *here*, but it is also changing all the time, and it is soon over and gone. Hegel accepts spatiality and temporality as the *particular* modes of Sense-Certainty that are immediately given, and he observes first the

transience of the sensible world. Our spatial world of singular
Things (I shall use the capital letter for *Sache* and "thing" for *Ding*),
is born for us each morning out of the darkness; Night and Day are
the two *specific* conditions of the sensible world. But they are *alter-
nating* states; if we say that it is *now* Night, the "now" implies that
daytime will come. We can keep Night (or Day) with us as a
memory, but not as a fact. What abides as a fact is the *Now* in which
the alternation occurs. The actual *Now* of conscious experience is
the universal receptacle of sensible change—and it is that receptacle which abides.

In the daytime, we are faced with a different mode of changing
content within an abiding universal form. This time the change is
voluntary; what we see from "here" depends upon which way we
choose to look. There is a tree in front of us and a house that is
invisible behind us, or vice versa. The elements of our speech that
refer to what "truly" (i.e., abidingly) is are all universal expressions. This is even true about the linguistic terms through which
we identify the non-linguistic Things that we "mean" (but which
we cannot *say* in language at all). It is true, for instance, about the
identification of the shimmering play of colours in our sunset.
"What is" is a set of universal linguistic forms that structure an
ineffably transient content.

That content is not *out there* in "the world" at all; it is in *my*
consciousness. The riches of Sense-Certainty are found in the way
that the world is "for me." This is the first "inversion" of our conscious position. Honesty drives us to try it, but, of course, it does
not enable us to grasp what "truly is." It only makes matters worse;
for every speaking consciousness, everyone who can say "I see
this," has the same right to say what she sees. Each of us has our
own personal world, but we can all share one another's worlds. If
I stand back to back with someone, she will see the house and I, the
tree. But we share the knowledge that both objects are there. Each
of us *remembers* what the other sees. My experience is not more
"real" than hers.

But suppose I insist that *my* actual experience standing firmly
here in the daylight is the paradigm of "true being." Can I say
exactly what is for me? When I use the relevant linguistic expressions to make a precise reference to "this that is here for me now,"
I am *pointing* at something. Can I do this with absolute precision?
The answer is that I can point *exactly* only at the cost of seeing

"what is" turn into "what is not"; "now" turns into "then," and "here" into "there." I can use "now" only as a pointer within the universal system of "thens"—the moments that *have been* but are not immediately present any longer. The moment that I point at is always a *then*. It still exists for me now, but it exists as a moment of the time that is *always* now, because it *has been*. And if I point out some place in space as "here," I must either point it out as "there" or point it out from some other place that is "there." Thus, what emerges as "true being" is not what immediately is at all, but the universal mediating and mediated system of what *essentially* is, in the "here and now" of the mind and its universal language, the here and now that is "always." The truth of immediate being is *essence*, and essence is what is *perceived* by the mind, not what is given immediately to the senses.

3. Perception

At the level of Sense-Certainty, we do not need to be philosophers at all; we *use* our language, but we *never* follow its "leading" towards the mental realm of *universal* concepts. When we become conscious *perceivers*, we have accepted that leading. We are no longer interested in what singular Things there are, but in what *kinds of thing* there are; and our philosophical question is "What does it *mean* to be a 'kind of thing'?"

All the transient impressions of sense now become the "properties" of the things. The "thing" can manifest itself to the perceiver in many different ways. The manifold content of the Now and the Here is all harmonized in it. What appears at one moment does not contradict what appears at another; it all exists together in the eternal "now and here" of the perceiver's mind.

The dialectical movement of Perception is far more complex than that of Sense-Certainty, because the subjective and objective moments of Consciousness are now as sharply distinguished as the levels of what "really is" and what "immediately appears." These two distinctions are not *identical*—though *identification* is one of the momentary positions in their motion. The sensory "this" now has a *real* status in addition to its immediate role as an appearance. This "reality" is its *essential* role as a "concept." The name "white" belongs to a *universal* property of things. The thing is a conceptual unity of many of these properties. A lump of salt is white, cubical, and "salty," for example: This view of it is the *positive* universality of the thing; it *contains* all of its properties in the space that it fills. As Hegel says, the thing is an *Also*; it is not only salty but *also* white, cubical, and so forth.

But a lump of sugar can be white too (though it need not be). When we describe the thing by listing its properties, every name derives its significance as much from what it denies as from what it asserts. The salt is white, *not* brown. The sugar is white (but it was probably brown at an earlier time in its history). Each lump, considered as a positive unit, is a negative (or exclusive) unity of a *particular* kind, because each property is both positive and negative. Assuming that the lumps now look very much alike, we can distinguish them only by taste; this will tell us the difference between them (as *singular* things) at once.

What we perceive immediately is the resemblance. One of my children once spoiled a bowl of strawberries and cream for me by putting salt in the sugar bowl. I did not enjoy the joke, but I knew very well that the error was *subjective*—it was *mine*. If I had tasted the white stuff first, I would have known better. But tasting is interesting because it abolishes the *thing* altogether; salt or sugar *in my mouth* returns to the transient flux of Sense-Certainty. This teaches us that Perception is *not* a passive "truth-taking" from the simple apprehension of the thing. The thing can be *known* only through its interactions with other things.

Tasting also powerfully supports the initial view that the *manifold* aspect of the thing's identity is only its "being-for-me." The *medium* of the "positive unity" is really "my mind." This view becomes problematic at once because, as a *singular* thing, the salt has that distinctive taste that *must* belong to it; and in order to be a thing-in-general (one that can be confused with others) it *must* have its other properties as well (however *accidental* they may be, like the whiteness of the refined sugar).

So we must try the opposite hypothesis, after all: The "thing" really *is* a collection of properties, and its unity arises from my intellectual activity of conception. I must conceive it as a community of powers that affect my senses. Whiteness, saltiness, and sweetness are really physical energies in the salt and sugar. Both of them are white throughout; to the eye they are the same. But one is sweet throughout and the other is salty; to the taste they are radically different. Their sensible properties are what Hegel calls "free matters." The visual white can go with the salty or the sweet taste.

This position is no more convincing than the first. The unity is as much "out there" in the thing as the "multiplicity," and if we suppose one to be really out there, the other has to be ascribed to the activity of perception. The philosophy of perception is a perpetual motion from one position to the other, in response to whatever pressures are put on the concept by its employment in experience. The "truth" of Perception is that the "thing-in-itself" is identical with the "thing-for-another." Every singular thing is "in itself" the totality of all of its possible relations with other things; and this identity exists for that crucial "other thing" for which the "thing-in-itself" necessarily exists: the perceiving mind. But, equally, the identity exists in the world. The world is the total system of the relatedness of things. Things both are and are not independent of (or separate from) one another in the world, just as their relatedness both is and is not in the mind. The finitude of things marks the advent of the universal system of relations. My tasting of the salt is emblematic of this fact. The salt is identified as what it *really is* precisely at the moment when it ceases to be anything but a transient impression in the cycle of sensible experience.

Every thing has its real ground in the whole system of things, but the *cognition* of things is like that too. All perception has its ground in the system of concepts. The story of the perceptual object is that first it turns into what Locke called my "ideas"; but these ideas are only *Vorstellungen*—representations of something supposed to be independently real. When they become fully *conceptual*, the concept is a contradiction, being both in the world and in the mind at the same time. When the shifting cycle is comprehended as a unity, we have passed over into the world of the Understanding. The world no longer consists of singular things, each each of which has its own essence. It is a universal order in which sense-consciousness is just the moment of manifestation. The *reality* is entirely intellectual. The *middle* moment (the world of finite things) drops out, and the great world process of temporal and spatial sensation returns, but now it is *comprehended*—instead of comprehending and engulfing us, its finite, would-be knowers.

Commonsense philosophy preserves itself because we need it in practice. "Things" are the elements that can be moved about freely. But we can preserve the illusion that this practical (external) standpoint is an adequate theory of cognition only by utilizing a great system of self-deceptive hypocrisy. All of our true perceptual statements are true only "relatively speaking" (or in a given context). In another context, we make an opposite set of assumptions and say quite the opposite things. If we really want to know what cognition is, we must bring the opposite positions together and find a way of seeing them as necessary aspects of a coherent viewpoint. Now we shall see how the Understanding achieves this goal.

4. Understanding

The concept of the *thing* suffered first a simple inversion into its direct antithesis: my representation of it as a unity of many sensible properties. Then came a comprehensive or double inversion of these two sides together, which united them into the higher concept of an intelligible world that manifests itself sensibly. The total process of cognition is now "unconditioned," or self-contained, because sensation has become simply a necessary moment (or phase) of the world's intellectual self-comprehension. Scientific cognition is *absolute* knowledge, because it is the way in which the world knows *itself* truly.

The Understanding is still a mode of simple consciousness. When we have *philosophical* understanding, we are clearly aware that we are *thinking* about a purely intelligible object. But the object is in the *world* not in our minds; to be more precise, the object is the intelligible foundation (or ground) of our real world. It existed *before* we were conscious of it at all, and it will continue to be just what it *is*, even if we fail to understand it. Our subjective understanding of it (insofar as we are successful) will be a duplication "in the intellect" of the Universal that already exists perfectly "in the thing" (as the medieval theorists put it). We are going to see how this "picture theory," this *Vorstellung* par excellence, transforms itself *for us* into a cyclic motion in which the Universal "in the thing" is united with the Universal "in the intellect." But this does not happen for the Understanding itself. The Understanding "posits" (or presupposes) the independence (the self-sufficient completeness) of its object *absolutely*. What happens for us can be made conscious for it too, but only as a subjective experience of *duplicating* "what truly is." It is *we*, who have *understood* Perception, who must from the beginning identify with the Concept, which the naive Understanding takes to be an independent, self-sufficient essence.

The perceptual thing and its properties became for us an intelligible form in which many "matters" were united, and in order to understand how *that* could be manifested *as* perception, we had to move to the concept of a unitary world of the necessary relations *between* things. This system of relations that are necessarily manifested is the real Concept of *Force(s)*. The manifestation is made *to us* as scientific perceivers. *Identifying* with the Concept at this stage means recognizing that "Science" is the true consciousness of the world as it is. Implicitly (insofar as we achieve true Understanding), we are the *self*-consciousness of the world. The objective Universal "in the thing" becomes *conscious of itself* in our minds. This is the coming to be of the Hegelian "Concept"; in Hegel's usage, the Concept signifies always something that *can* be—and is logically destined to become—*conscious of itself*. It is not (properly, or in its fully developed shape) an *object* of the mind, but an *act*. The Understanding *posits* it as an object, because the finite consciousness does not see how it could possibly be the *self*-consciousness of anything but its own *finite* self. But if we think that "the mind" could possibly belong to the finite consciousness as a personal (or "private") possession, we are gravely mistaken. The logical truth of "experience" (from the first) is that "the mind" can only be known to *exist* in the finite consciousness; what the mind *is* (or *can be* as a fully realized essence) we must find out by observation. But since it can only exist in the finite consciousness, we must freely surrender that consciousness to the bare concept of the intellect at this point, in order to *let it be* whatever it truly is.

From now on, therefore, we are the evolving self-consciousness of the scientific concept of *Force*. The perceptual world is the utterance (*Äusserung*), the spreading out (*Ausbreitung*) of Force in space and time; and Force (*Kraft*) is the real Concept that logically *must* manifest itself as this world of relations (always partly explicit and partly hidden). In order to *be* manifest, this *real* concept must be "solicited" by itself as intellect; so, in order to be the real concept, Force *must* duplicate itself as the two "universals" (objective in the thing and subjective in the intellect). This is not the Berkeleyan idealism of perception, because the intellect has an "eternal" standpoint. We understand that there *were* dinosaurs and—more tentatively—there was a Big Bang, there will be a cold Sun and a dead planet. Hegel knew none of these things. What this says about his "identity" with the Concept (and ours) we shall realize in due course. With the evolution of the Concept, this problem is not so much solved as dissolved.

According to the Concept, the soliciting activity of the perceiving mind is just a duplication of the force that manifests itself. Each side both solicits and is solicited. The perceived world is the *result* of this perfect complementarity. The two forces vanish into their middle term. But the vanishing is properly the activity of Understanding, for we are not *satisfied* with the perceived world; we cannot comprehend it in that simple mode without contradiction. It is the complementary movement of our conceptual Understanding that comes to rest in the "unconditioned Universal" by bringing the subjective concept back to its true identity with the objective concept that was our perceptual problem.

It is the structure of this "return" that is the principal topic of Hegel's chapter. The mind looks through the perceptual appearance into the supersensible world. We compose the changing show of sense-perception into a pattern of *appearance* which is recognizable as the manifest shape of a *law*. Thus, the supersensible world is the true theoretical *interpretation* of the sensible world. Heracleitus intuitively recognizes the motion of the Sun in its "measures" as the Logos that we must all heed. But we must quantify the "measures" if we are to understand the Logos. Force and Utterance are logically identical. Behind the pattern of appearance lies a permanently stable set of equations; the mathematical structure is present in the order of motion and change as a kind of still picture. But no matter how much of the order we manage to grasp in our concepts, there is always more change and novelty that we have not yet comprehended; and as soon as we have a multiplicity of discovered "laws," we must try to correlate them, to weave them into a conceptual *system*.

When Newton saw how the "free" motion of the Moon (its cyclic "infinity") fitted into the same universal theory that accounted for the finite motion of the falling apple, the Understanding made its greatest advance, because all motions came together under one Concept. But Gravity—as the principle of universal *attraction*—is only the bare concept of universal law. Like the concept of Force, that Gravity must be *othered* in its complement—the principle of universal repulsion. From the motion of the Moon nobody can tell what will happen to the apple when it hits the earth, and the "law of Gravity" does not yet contain all the distinctions that belong to a fully developed concept, because attraction and repulsion are only externally related. Electricity and magnetism reveal more adequately the actual structure of the concept of law.

But the multiplicity of forces (and their "laws") remains a problem. As an "explanation," the law remains only a "tautologous" duplication of the apparent pattern. To have identified the pattern is not a trivial thing, but when we find that the discovered laws fit into a broader theory, we realize that the "tautology" involved is of a speculative kind. Hegel is only underlining the fact that the scientific explanation logically *must* be *identical* with the objective Concept that is here expressed in words and equations. Drawing attention to this tautological relation is like complaining that formal syllogisms cannot give us any new knowledge. What is *true* is that the kind of identity that is formally necessary is not adequate for the self-conceiving of our own Reason in its free activity. The Understanding must operate by this standard because it has not recognized itself as the true "inwardness" of things. It takes itself to be only an external observer.

"Tautology" only appears to be trivial and worthless because, in our mathematical model of the order of Nature, everything is *still*. But the world we are explaining is in motion. The Universal in things is alive and active; this truth begins to emerge when we examine the language of our theories. Attraction and repulsion are not really independent and separate concepts (as they appear to be in abstraction). The *North* pole of the magnet is the one that attracts its opposite (in this same magnet) and *repels* "itself" in any other magnet. The "self-sameness" that is universally attractive must equally be "self-repulsive" if there is to be a world at all. Thus, our supersensible world of laws in a state of eternal rest must be recognized to contain its own opposite—the active principle of eternal motion. This "second supersensible world" is important because it brings us back necessarily to the sphere of Perception. It is natural and easy to think of the still world of laws as a supersensible Beyond, but when we are asked to admit that the North pole conceptually contains the South pole, we must think of the actual magnet; and when Hegel suggests that the sweet taste should be conceptualized as containing "sour," he is reaching back to the "porosity" of the "matters" in Perception. *White* and *sweet* do contain one another in sugar. Of course, it is not *natural* to suppose that "sour" is actually sweet "inside" (in the way that South and North must be inside each other if they are to be comprehended as a "force" that causes motion). Hegel admits that we do not *have* to take the "inverted world" in this naive way. The example is brought in only to show us where the *inversion* takes us (i.e., back to Perception).

Hegel can illustrate the "inverted world" fully as an experience only by moving far ahead into the social world of the Spirit. Here the three worlds can be observed as a succession of distinct states (each of which involves its predecessor[s]). In the tribal society of natural feeling, Justice appears as the balanced alternation of the family feud. This is a perceptual *contradiction* that is resolved by the establishment of social authority. The law of Justice is now found in the motionless world of the intellect, and to try to keep the swaying balance moving is itself a crime that has to be nullified. But in the higher sphere of *absolute* spirit, the judicial function of pardon (the freedom of justice from simple "tautology" or equivalence) becomes the universal duty of forgiveness; and the cross upon which the worst of malefactors is executed becomes the symbol of divine love.

This higher example is only important to us here, because all the stages are shown to be present in our earthly existence, and nowhere else. The "beyond" of criminal justice exists only in our shared commitment to identify criminals and punish them as *fairly* as possible. Otherwise, "the law" is only an abstraction. This directs our minds to the fact that the Earth itself is the absolute magnet, the "infinite" context of all our finite magnets. At the level of theoretical Understanding (as a mode of "consciousness"), magnetism is the only clear example that Hegel has. But the weird suggestion that sweetness must be inwardly sour is pedagogically justified because it teaches us how we ought to think about sensation (and its linguistic expressions).

5. The Infinite

With the comprehension of Appearance as the necessary self-inversion of the supersensible world of natural law, the evolution of the Understanding is complete. The Unconditioned Universal has successfully absorbed the whole sphere of relational conditions; it stands before us in its self-sufficient independence or its "Infinity." *We* know that its whole cycle is the motion of our own universal intelligence; we understand that "natural science" is the self-comprehension of Force. But even the naive Understanding that we are observing knows that the second (comprehensive) inversion is true and necessary. For every scientific intelligence knows that it (and its realm of subjective experience) is somehow embraced within and comprehended by the world that is known to it as an intelligible order of law. It may suppose that it is itself known to the "Author of Nature" in quite a different way from that in which it comes to know the natural order. But its own way of knowing is part of the order. In *our* comprehension there is no room for the "Author of Nature." Our way of knowing *is* the way in which knowing comes to be the climax of the order itself. It is the fundamental *law* of the order that it should know itself. The law of nature is the conceptual unity of identity (attraction, Understanding) and distinction (self-repulsion, Appearance). This unity is the Concept that Hegel calls *Life*. The "Life" of which he speaks here is God's *eternal* life, the universal or divine life. If we try to *imagine* God as a self-knowing consciousness *beyond* the first supersensible world that the Understanding spontaneously and necessarily posits, this version of the "second inversion" will pose an insoluble problem for us. We have to ask, "*Why* did the Absolute go out of itself?" (and *how* does it do so?). Why does the "Author of Nature" *need* Nature at all, and how does "He" know it, and us in it?

Our own progress within the Concept of Force as it comes to Understanding has shown us that this is a pseudo-problem. The Absolute does not "go out" of itself into finitude at all. The finite world is a moment in its own process. It must come to itself out of finitude and return to comprehend its finitude as its own "Infinity." Our coming to Understanding *is* the divine self-Understanding, and our finite, mortal life *is* the divine Life. "The consciousness of an other . . . is itself necessarily Self-consciousness" says Hegel (W. and C. 118:6–8; Miller ¶164). It is easy to overlook the fact that this assertion only follows logically at this point, if the "Self-Consciousness" is that of the absolute Self, the Self that all the finite selves must be and must share. *Then*, if we focus our minds upon the scientific knowledge of the world, the transition is

quite simple. But the empirical implications of this insight are stag-
gering. *Self*-Consciousness, Hegel is saying, can only exist *at all* in
a community of finite world-consciousnesses. We are mistaken, in
the Protagorean moment of our Sense-Certainty, when we think
that we can (and do) each have a private world that is independent
of the others. We have private worlds (and experiences), but they
are not, and *cannot* be, independent. For even the supposed absolute consciousness (the Author of Nature) *cannot* be a "Self-Consciousness." God, in his loneliness, is not a self. The cycle from the
finite to the infinite Life (and back again) is *necessary* to all Self-
Consciousness.

We shall now move on to observe a "self" that does not know
any of this. All of this is "forgotten"; the self we observe *presupposes* all of it because it takes itself to *be* the absolute self. The world
belongs to it. But it does not know what we know about selfhood;
and it must find its way painfully into a *relation* with the absolute
self that is different from (and *opposite* to) the identity-relation
from which it begins.

The transition is necessary because the self-cognition of the Infinite has been shown to depend on the community of finite living
consciousness. The free spontaneity of the living consciousness
(from which the movement of Understanding and, indeed, of
Sense-Certainty began) is the one thing that cannot be comprehended within the *tautological* Concept of the Understanding. The
Understanding can understand everything except its own existence. The necessity that it understands is the necessity of its own
freedom, and that is incomprehensible.

Chapter 5
Self-Consciousness

1. The Truth of Self-Certainty

The climax of "Consciousness" in the Infinite is a point at which several paths meet. Hegel makes it clear that we could go straight on from the comprehension of scientific Understanding to develop the "system of Science" itself—that is, we could begin at once with pure Logic (see W. and C. 117:32–33; Miller ¶164). Instead, there appears a new *Gestalt* of consciousness that knows nothing of the experience through which we have gone. Also, we have completed a circle at this point, since we can recognize the Infinite Life as the great cycle of time in which Sense-Certainty knows itself to be engulfed at the very beginning. This is the first explanation that Hegel offers us of how "the Absolute is with us from the start" (compare W. and C. 58:7–12 and 116:27–32; Miller ¶¶ 73 and 163). The Understanding can remain content in its subjectively organized world, gazing at the curtain behind which it supposes the "Author of Nature" to have his habitation—or perhaps only Absolute Matter is there. The mystery must simply be accepted (or the blank must be filled by "Faith").

This is not the path that we shall follow or the "station" at which we can halt. We must continue to identify ourselves with the universal Concept of Life that has emerged; and we must observe the emergence from it of the singular independent self which has none of the knowledge that we have gained by experience, but which knows instinctively that it is at home in the world that belongs to it by natural right. The story of theoretical "necessity" it has quite "forgotten" (or has never learned); but it knows that it is *free*.

This certainty that "the world is mine" is the "native land of truth." It will give place to the certainty that "the world is the Lord's" before it can be reformulated rationally as "the world is ours." But with Self-Consciousness, we have reached the absolute position to which we shall finally return after making a great circle.

The natural self with which we begin knows quite well that the world is something other than itself, but that otherness is not its "truth."

Its "truth" is the world's *destiny*, which is to be made over into the mirror of the self as Desire. Truth is still an "essence" (though we cannot say that its *eternal* status is recognized), for it is not what immediately is, but rather the "Heart's Desire"; and that is what it will remain for a long time, before we return to do justice to the Infinite of Understanding. At present, the truth of Understanding has a merely instrumental status.

2. Desire and Life

This natural self is alive. Its desire presents itself first in the objective shape of the living body and the family within which its finite life is generated and sustained. This body (and family) must be kept satisfied and happy, but in the natural servitude of Desire, the self discovers that its own true goal is to be free. Hence it will attempt to reduce even its own body to the status of an instrument that can be sacrificed, and it will discover that its life is an "independent being" that cannot be reduced to a mere instrument.

Before we can embark on this journey, however, we must make the transition properly. In the final movement of the Understanding, we reached the Divine Life. The Infinite of Understanding is realized in the great world-order of the Solar System; within that system, it is the Earth—"pure axial rotation" (W. and C. 122:37; Miller ¶169)—that sustains all life, and that life is a community of members who subsist for a finite time. The community is made up of families which subsist indefinitely because their singular members come together with the required sexual complements. The moments of the life-cycle are, first, the nutrition and growth of the two sexes as individuals; next, they are caught up in the process by which Life reproduces itself; and, finally, the new individual life comes to birth with its own sexual determination. The new baby is the central focus of family life, and as it grows to maturity it discovers its own independent self-consciousness.

The natural evolution of the self as Desire follows a similar pattern, but its goal is independent selfhood. It is a conscious negative. In the moment of its bodily nutrition and growth, it becomes the consumer who devours everything and so gains the objective certainty of its own "truth." But the satisfaction is only momentary. Life is experienced as the perpetual rebirth of Desire, and the negative freedom of consumption is soon recognized as bondage to the needs of finite life. In order to be free, the living self needs another *consciousness* that can stand between it and its instinctual drives. That other (being mature, and also ministering to its needs) presents it objectively with the image of "another self" that it can take as its goal. In the order of natural life, this is the educational function of parents. Boys want to be like their fathers, girls like their mothers. It is in this imitative activity that freedom is first effectively discovered and realized; and in this relationship the concept of self-conscious Spirit is born. The self is implicitly spirit from the first—as the project of "recognizing itself in absolute otherness" (compare W. and C. 19:22 and 121:15–37; Miller ¶¶ 26 and 167); but with the identification of a desired self, the Concept of Spirit is explicitly before us: "the I that is We, and We that is I" (W. and C. 127:23–24; Miller ¶177). Spirit is self-conscious identity in the community of equals.

3. The Concept of Recognition

The bare Concept of Spirit is the concept of Self-Recognition in the Other. The *experience* of it will at first be one of *inequality*. We shall pass from the recognition of a human Lord to the recognition of God as the Absolute Lord. But we have discovered the Concept of Spirit in the *ideal* shape of the process of education as the Truth of Desire. There must necessarily be inequality between the self that I am and that which I want to be, but the inequality is strictly momentary. It belongs necessarily to the character of selfhood as free purpose. The *goal* is to establish equality. Recognition is a conceptual unity of opposites. But it is obvious what this means: The dialectical resolution of the opposition is as spontaneous as the actual expression of life itself.

When I recognize someone else in the self that I want to be but am not, then (logically) two opposite things happen at once. I must be in a (very *metaphysical*) state of "despair" because my own self is lost to me. It is out there in this objective *other*. But also, by the very logic of Self-Consciousness, that objective other is sublated into a merely instrumental status. It is I who am going to *be* what the other self only *represents*. In *equal* recognition, the sublation, like the despair, becomes purely metaphysical. But that is not how they are experienced initially.

If it truly is myself that I see in the other, then I cannot want to see the other self perish in the world when it is actualized in me. The logic of self-recognition dictates that my own success must be marked by the releasing of the model self whom I have copied back into the free existence that I have achieved through her, and that spontaneous freedom must characterize every step of the self-realization process. Recognition is not like simple Desire, because nothing can be done to (or with) the other that she does not do to herself. Each of us must see the other doing the same thing that we do ourselves (i.e., not the same thing in content, but the same thing in form: acting *freely*). The logic of Self-Consciousness as Desire (to which I have just appealed) actually sublates itself here. For the *instrumental* status of the other is a mere show; it is "true" in both directions and in neither. The mutually soliciting and solicited relation in the "play" of Forces is repeated at this higher level. We recognize ourselves as mutually recognizing each other.

This is the concept as we see it unfolding in ordinary life. It is realized everywhere in the happy family, when the children join their parents in the world of mature beings. But in the experience of the singular consciousness facing the Infinite of Consciousness in freedom, the emergence of the Concept is more painful. The natural self takes possession of the world quite spontaneously as the instrument of its desires; it only discovers *freedom* as an objective goal to be achieved when it encounters another self that is doing the same thing. In the immediate experience of self-recognition, both the despair and the sublation are fully *actual*. When I see *him*, I have both found and lost myself in the same instant, and I can recover this newfound self only by wiping the other out absolutely. Actually, of course, the experience is *not* immediate. I do not *see* my freedom in him. I discover what my freedom is and means by trying to determine *whether* he is free (as I take myself to be).

Logically, this is a question that can be settled only by fighting to the death. Empirically, this does happen in the warfare of the extended families called "tribes." But Hegel has abstracted the experience from all "life-contexts" because he wants us to see that simple freedom as an abstract immediate goal is contradictory precisely because it is *empty*. If the battle does go to the death, the one who survives has no mirror in which to know himself; and in the perfect case in which both of us die, the proving of the "truth" is the demonstration of its absolute futility. Only the outside observers learn, and what they learn is that freedom must be found *within* life.

4. Lordship and Bondage

The emergent contradiction in the concept of Freedom can be resolved only by the voluntary sharing out of the two "sides" (subordination to life and free self-expression). This happens spontaneously when one of the combatants surrenders in the battle and is granted life upon the condition of life-service. But the spontaneity is typically logical rather than real, because it is usually a whole community that accepts subjection. For individuals the transition is simply "necessary"; they have no choice in the matter. The real Lord in the relationship is Death, which becomes the *inevitable* consequence of disobedience, rather than the uncertain outcome of an equal contest.

In the new relation Self-Consciousness is *actual*, because each member has another visible self. The serf beholds in his Lord the freedom that he knows to be his own essence as human; but the mode of his beholding bars him necessarily from the fulfilment of his Desire, because its object is his Lord, who represents only certain death if the *sublation* is attempted. Here the moment of *self-loss* is perfectly frozen. What is *new* as a result is the relation of *labour*. In the natural community of Life, there was already labour to satisfy desire; but labour *proper* is working upon another's things to bring them into accordance with *his* desire. The thing-world ceases to be merely instrumental; it now has an independent status that must be respected.

The Lord is "free" in an obvious sense, but the recognition-relation is incomplete because he does not do to himself what he does to his serf. He has made the serf recognize and accept subservience to Life, but he does not do that himself. He has reduced the serf to subservient dependence and obedience, so all that he can behold in him is the truth of his own dependence upon bodily life. ✓

It is the serf who can discover a new shape of freedom in his experience. He is the master of nature in quite a new way. He is only an observer of what both master and serf regard as true freedom. But labouring under the restriction of absolute respect for what he labours on (as the property of his Lord) gives him the first experience of *creative* freedom. His Lord gives the orders, but the serf has to interpret them for himself, in the light of what is best for the world that he works on. He becomes a craftsman (the first of his crafts being agriculture). There were *free* craftsmen in the natural community of families. But according to Hegel's logical analysis, labouring always in the shadow of a life-and-death authority is crucially important, because that is how we learn to remake ourselves. If we followed always the path of natural Desire—discovering our ideal self in another and schooling ourselves into it willingly—we should never discover our *rational* capacity to make ourselves from nothing. The fear of the human Lord is a preparation for the fear of God, which is the true "beginning of wisdom." To achieve the freedom of the Spirit, we must make an *absolute* break with nature. That is why the "first experience" of Self-Consciousness is the self-identification of those who are willing to go to their natural death for the sake of their freedom. They are the first agents of spiritual freedom. = slaves

5. Stoicism and Scepticism

The future development of the new freedom discovered by the serf lies far ahead upon our logical journey. We shall come to it only in the world of *Bildung* (Culture); the universalization of serfdom to the Divine Lord (in a *perfectly* voluntary mode) will be necessary for its further evolution. At the moment, our progression involves the uniting of the two sides in a singular consciousness. This transition *can* occur on either side of the Lordship/ Bondage relationship, and logically it must occur on both sides at once. The Lord must recognize the servitude implicit in his doing nothing but give orders about the reorganization of Nature; and the serf must recognize the freedom involved in his giving "his own sense" to everything that he does. When these sides are brought together, we have *Stoicism*—the philosophy for which the actual social position of the individual is of no import. "On the throne" (with Marcus Aurelius) or "in fetters" (with Epictetus), one retains the "freedom of thought" that is essentially human (W. and C. 138:31–32; Miller ¶199).

Here, for the first time, the logic of consciousness becomes determinately *historical*. Stoicism and Scepticism belong to the Hellenistic world in which Rome eventually emerged as the Imperial Power. From this fixed point we can locate Lordship and Bondage in the *political* system of the Greek Cities (with Eteocles and Polyneices as the paradigm of the struggle to the death). The serfdom of the Feudal System is the "returned" shape of Lordship and Bondage under the universal aegis of the Divine Lord (in the Unhappy Consciousness). *Actual* freedom is entirely absent from this classical and medieval world; for even in the Greek Cities what we recognize as "individual freedom" in the full sense does not exist. (We shall see why this is so when we come to "True Spirit.")

Stoic freedom of thought depends entirely upon a retreat from the actual world. Epictetus is as free as Marcus, and Marcus is fettered by his social function. The singular freedom of the natural Self-Consciousness is completely sublated; thought lets Nature go free (as at the end of the speculative Logic). But this means that free thought has no content; it can produce only formal tautologies and abstract logical inferences. Any content that this thinking has must be picked up from experience; and the Sceptics therefore begin to argue convincingly that no empirical assumptions can be justified against their contradictories.

Stoicism unites the Lord/Bondsman Concept into the thought of independence; Scepticism *realizes* this independence as a dialectical freedom from reality. We have to admit *absolutely* that we know nothing. Every positive thesis of the Stoics about the universal government of cosmic Reason in the world can be balanced by an equally convincing argument for the corresponding negative thesis. The freedom of thought is found only in the suspense of judgement. The freedom of thought implies the freedom of Nature. Having been let go, Nature must be left in its freedom. (We should notice that it is in Scepticism that the reciprocity of equal Recognition is fully realized for the first time).

Scepticism is a great turning point. It is the self-conscious awareness of the same dialectic that has kept us moving all through Consciousness, and it can only assume a dominant role in the intellectual world after the emergence of the singular will as Lord of the World has shown that there is no "law of Nature" in the realm of the Spirit. Hegel claims that it was the ancient Sceptics who exposed the "sophistry" by which Perception maintains itself as an objective standard of knowledge.

But the *untroubled* condition that Scepticism achieves is a sham. The Sceptic can prove to the Stoic that he is the plaything of Fate only because they both are. Real life is merely a maelstrom of animal impulses and irrational passions. If the rational Stoic is actually a lost soul, his Sceptical adversary is no better off. Scepticism experiences Self-Consciousness as contradiction, but it does not bring the sides of the contradiction together in its own life. The Stoic, trying heroically to "follow Reason" and "love Fate," is a comic figure. But the *real* absence of law and justice in the world is no comedy. When the Sceptical consciousness begins to reflect upon its own condition as the sublation of Stoicism (not just its negation), its happy laughter turns into supreme unhappiness.

6. The Unhappy Consciousness

Kojève began an influential tradition in which the Lordship/ Bondage relation is regarded as the most fundamental "experience of consciousness." This view is mistaken, but there is a nugget of true insight in it. The *Phenomenology is* the story of the evolution of the recognition-relation from absolute inequality to absolute equality, but the Lordship/Bondage relation is *not* the extreme of absolute inequality. When Hegel speaks (in the Preface) of "*pure* self-cognition in absolute otherness" (W. and C. 19:22; Miller ¶26), he is referring to the finite/infinite relation, or to our relation with God or Nature as "Spirit." This is the extreme that we have now reached. Among the pioneering French interpreters it was Jean Wahl who grasped this point, not Kojève. Kojève's own (essentially "Enlightened") ontology forced him to regard "Absolute Spirit" as "ideology" (i.e., as what Hegel calls *Vorstellung*). He did not grasp the point that social identification and *universal* selfhood are more fundamental than natural identity and singular selfhood; he did not understand that Self-Consciousness is *never* immediately singular. So his whole interpretation (in spite of its many insights) is radically distorted.

"*Pure* self-cognition in absolute otherness" is the exact description of the Unhappy Consciousness, the pole of spiritual *despair*. This self is the unity of two absolutely opposed selves. The Stoic God (of which all finite selves are "sparks") has returned into the Sceptical Consciousness which knows for certain that we are absolutely cut off from this "absolute knowledge." The finite self is rational in the Stoic way; Carneades the Sceptic accepts all of the ideals and standards of the Stoic Chrysippus (from whose voluminous writings he got the arguments for the positive side of his dialectic). But this ideal of Reason has *no* viable connection with his finite existence—and now that he has stopped being a professor in retreat from the world, that knowledge has become *tragic*.

The Spirit has come to *life* and returned to actual existence (i.e., not just to the real world, but to the attempt to manifest its essence in the world). The attempt only reveals the contradiction. The finite self identifies itself as a moment caught up in the great river of the transient world; and it *projects* its own universal Reason into the Beyond as an Unchangeable Consciousness. (This projection is an act of "faith" which radically differentiates the unhappy consciousness from both the Stoic and the Sceptic, who both *know* about the Absolute, but in opposite ways.)

The goal is the unity of the Changeable Consciousness with the Unchangeable. But this goal is unattainable, because the finite consciousness is now the awareness of self-assertion as sinful. Even to be united with the Unchangeable is a self-assertive project. Life can be only a perpetual act of repentance for living; and the contradiction can only be overcome by a movement from the side of the Unchangeable. Since it *is* the Unchangeable, the movement has to be a progressive revelation of what it is, was, and always will be.

At this point, it becomes apparent that the experience we are now observing is that of Catholic Christendom (in the *Gestalt* of a typical illiterate layperson). The *movement* of the Unchangeable is that of God's Incarnation as the Universal Saviour. The Unchangeable is revealed first as the Father, Lord and Judge of the Old Testament. Many interpreters have followed Wahl in calling this phase "Judaism," but that is a mistake because Judaism is not a shape of the *Weltgeist*. It was the *Christian inheritance* of the Jewish Scriptures that became a universal experience, and it became universal only as *recollection*, during the *second* phase of the Unhappy Consciousness. Hegel warns us that the Unchangeable in and for itself has not yet arisen for us, and that its experience will be rather different from that of the singular consciousness with which we are presently concerned (W. and C. 146:15–21; Miller ¶211).

In our present object, the second phase, the Unchangeable becomes another *finite* self, opposed to the lost unhappy self; and, finally, in the third phase the two selves (infinite and finite) will be reconciled. But Hegel's fourth chapter deals only with the second phase. For the Changeable Consciousness, God's becoming a man is an *event*; but in order for the man to be truly God, the contradiction between finite mortality and infinite life must have been sublated by the completion of the finite moment in death far away and long ago. God's human embodiment is now with the Unchangeable in its own place. We must live here in the hope of joining him when we pass through the portal of death.

Our life in Christ while we are here has three aspects: first, there is the reverent devotion in Church, where we contemplate the miracle of the Mass; second, there is our weekday existence of desire and labour; and, third, there is our Sunday awareness of salvation (the dawning of the third phase but not yet its comprehensive fulfillment).

Devotion (*Andacht*—the experience of God in pure thought) is something more than mere reflective thought yet less than actual speculative thinking. With respect to the latter, Hegel puns upon the German word, saying that the devout consciousness comes to the threshold of thought (*Denken*) but cannot cross it (W. and C. 148:28–34; Miller ¶217). All of Scholastic philosophy and theology uses the reflective logic of simple Consciousness, just as the Stoics do. But, in principle, the Unhappy Consciousness is beyond that, because it does not turn its back on the concrete singularity of real life and retreat into the sphere of abstract universality. Devotion is a kind of *Vorstellung* in action of the speculative thinking that begins from its own *existence*. Devotion observes *and participates in* the miracle of God's Incarnation. In the Mass, the God Man is seen and touched, but at the same time the encounter occurs in thought. Both parties are in the intellectual realm, but their meeting is a speechless communion of sound without sense. When the miracle happens a bell is rung. This shapeless sound falls short of thought; it makes only a mute contact possible. In the world of our lives, God is dead. He has left us only a grave, an empty tomb to fight about. That battle itself is hopeless; only after defeat is accepted can the quest for salvation in actual thinking properly begin.

When the devout consciousness leaves the Church after the *service*, it enters upon its own part in the movement that has begun on the side of the Unchangeable. Being a self, it *must* assert itself. But it does so negatively. It *finds* itself alive, so it sets itself to deny its identity with this life. But this is a contradiction, because it must make the denial *in life*. It is *broken* into two sides: serving God and labouring for its own enjoyment. The objective world of its consciousness is broken, too: The world is the *instrument* of Self-Consciousness (the Unchangeable), but equally it is hallowed everywhere by God's saints. It is God's own shape, and even the labouring power that works upon it is his gift. But it is we who enjoy the benefit of these gifts. It is by God's will that we exist as free agents, and we possess nothing but the surface that he surrenders for our use and enjoyment. But when we give it all back to him in our thanksgiving, this is "broken" too. Our thanks give back only what we have fully enjoyed. Reflection into God (as the essence) is equally reflection into the finite self. Ultimately, labour and thanksgiving are inadequate. We must repent for the selfish lives we lead.

Our *repentance* is not a simple return to the beginning of "devotion," for we have come now to the penitence by which we receive "absolution." The penitent seeks to make an effective demonstration of her own nothingness. She can be united with God only if she wipes out her own independent consciousness. Like Luther struggling with the Devil in the shape of his own constipation ("the animal functions"), the penitent self can see herself from God's point of view. Through this awareness she can be united with God. But now a mediating consciousness is needed to assure the penitent that her animal existence of desire, labour, and elimination is all necessary and in accordance with the will of God.

The mediator must tell me what to do, so that the doing, enjoying, and responsibility are not mine. His speech is only moral advice, for I must come voluntarily to God and give myself up. I renounce even my consciousness at the linguistic level, for I perform my divine service in a language that I do not know (and if I am literate, my literacy gives me only the knowledge that what I say expresses incomprehensible mysteries). Thus, I turn my own consciousness into a thing (the mechanical memory) and give it to God. Like almsgiving and penitential fasting, the whole action is symbolic. But my confessor can tell me that everything is the Will of God and that I am absolved. Thus, my hopeless struggle, which never reaches any objective fulfilment, does in fact create the *authority* of the Church and the reality of God's will in the world. My experience of salvation is postponed, but the *Vorstellung* of it is complete; and as the sublation in principle of my unhappiness, this is the *Vorstellung* of Reason. I come to my reconciliation with God through the mediation of another penitent sinner like myself. All of it is a miracle produced by the movement of the Unchangeable itself, and what arises from the experience is the authority of the Church, not any objective consciousness of my own Reason. But when this realized object becomes my own subjective experience, I shall be subjective *Reason*—conscious unity with my God.

Chapter 6
Reason

1. The Certainty and Truth of Reason

Between the last sentence of Hegel's fourth chapter and the first sentence of the fifth, we take an enormous step forward. Self-Consciousness moves from the objective *Vorstellung* of itself to the pure thought of itself, the *Gedanke*. Empirically, this is a lengthy and complex movement. We go from the Mass and the confessional all the way to Fichte's self-positing Ego. The figure of Fichte is easily recognized in the characterization of "Idealism" with which the fifth chapter begins. But when we look at the *end* of the chapter, we can identify Kant with equal certainty. So Fichte is here at the beginning, because his theory is also where the circle closes; and the actual thread of the development that leads to him begins with Bacon and Descartes (who can fairly be said to be reconciled in Kant's Critical Philosophy). The chapter begins with the shape of subjective Reason in its fully self-conscious critical form, but the serial evolution of Consciousness continues with our observation of "instinctive" Reason (in the "Observation of Nature").

The Unhappy Consciousness sublates (or supersedes) its own self-will by freely alienating itself from its own spontaneous self-expression. Through this supersession of its own self-will, it establishes the free self as the universal identity of thought and being (though only in the alienated shape of Church authority as the will of God on Earth). In Bacon this "Will of God" becomes the conscious will of "Man"; and in Descartes the symbolic "union with God" that is always postponed beyond the grave becomes the experience of Reason here and now in this thinking life. Reason is "the certainty of being all truth" (W. and C. 157:25–26; Miller ¶231), and we can see that this is a reference to the *Cogito* of Descartes when Hegel connects the dawn of "Idealism" with the end of the Crusades ("the grave of its truth") and the Reformation

47

("the abolishing of the abolition of its actuality" [W. and C. 158:5–12; Miller ¶232]).

Having made this chronological connection, Hegel looks the other way around the circle of rational experience and offers a rapid characterization of Fichtean Idealism. Fichte's self-positing Ego comes to itself in the immediate present, as if it had no past. It has forgotten the Self of Lordship and the God of Stoicism; and it is unintelligible to the Enlightened common sense, which has adopted the same idealistic position in its Baconian "instinctive" fashion. Fichte's idealism does not comprehend itself and cannot make itself comprehensible. This is a problem to which Hegel returns in the Preface (W. and C. 20:4–21; Miller ¶26), and we can see there that it is the problem of the whole book, but it is also, more immediately, the problem of this fifth chapter: to exhibit Fichtean idealism as the logical climax of the modern era that began with the Renaissance.

In Fichte's speculative organization of the Critical Philosophy, the Ego becomes the *category* of all Being. Kant's table of twelve categories logically evolves out of it. (Hegel may mean to refer to his own categorical logic here, but it is Kant's theory that is before the public, and Hegel had shown how that could be "Fichteanized" in *Faith and Knowledge*.) The singular consciousness, in and for which this evolution occurs, *excludes* both the pure category and the plurality of particular categories. It is the consciousness of its own existence, in the context of the world as eternal. But the cognition of the world refers us again to the universal Ego and its system of particular categories. We can still recognize the Sceptical division here. Rational consciousness is a quest for itself in the not-self. It *is* the whole process, in which it also *appears* to itself as the opposed terms. The Idealist position identifies the rational self with the "pure category," but this formal idealism is equally a radical empiricism. Through Fichte's evident allegiance to Locke (satirized, almost, in *Faith and Knowledge*), Hegel can make the necessary transition to the "instinctive" Idealism of the scientific empiricists. The contradiction in Critical Idealism, represented by Kant's *Ding an sich* (or the Fichtean *Anstoss*), arises because the "pure Category" is taken to be what truly is in its abstract independence. Reason thus condemns itself to a "bad infinite" quest—that is, one that has no terminus in which it finds itself. But our own "observing Reason" will comprehend what happens. We *are* the speculative Idealism that advances from Reason's certainty to its "truth."

This summary of a very dense and difficult passage in Hegel's text may not make things clear for a beginning reader, but nothing better can be provided in a bird's-eye view. This is one point in the argument at which the reader can only be told to study the background history of German idealism and to read the rest of Hegel's book (and of this book) before coming back to Hegel's discussion at this point and trying again to see if things have improved.

2. Observation of Nature

Rational Observation initially *appears* to be simply a *self-conscious return* to the standpoint of Consciousness, but Reason is seeking its own closure into "infinity." Reason is *beyond* the level of the Understanding, even when it seems to be still far short of the "supersensible world." It begins by taking possession of the sensible world at what looks like the level of naive Perception. Observation is the matching of *concepts* with sense-perceptions, and Observing Reason is consciously concerned with the essence of "things," not with itself; but it knows that its things are actual concepts. First, it observes "Nature" (as a living system, not as a mechanical/chemistic system of forces); next, Spirit, and finally their connection as soul and body.

Both the first and the third phases of this movement (and particularly the first) are discussed at much greater length than is necessary. But if we keep a tight hold on the fact that it is the "life" of Nature as a whole that is the *object* of Rational Observation, we shall be able to understand what happens. Observation develops in step with its object, so we shall be observing some aspects of the advance of what empirical scientists call "scientific method." But that is *not* what this section is about—just as it is not about the description and classification of *things*, although that is where it seems to begin.

The actual beginning is with Perception as a rational concept. Description and classification are endless tasks. We pursue them to the point where we do not know whether the details observed are significant; in this uncertainty, we must be guided by the way in which things distinguish themselves. They only do this properly as animal organisms. Moving downwards from there, we eventually find a fluid continuum, and we realize that we *cannot* make a conceptual system that *mirrors* the order of Nature.

From this perceptual (or passively receptive) observation, we are driven on to the rational Understanding of what lies beneath the surface of appearance. We begin to act upon Nature experimentally, to discover what is not directly observable. This is the *experience* of Observation as a formal concept. It inverts the concept of observation as such, because it is based upon the *action* and the *thoughtful control* of the investigator, who wants to construct a *theory* of what underlies the observable reality. Reason is *instinctive* at this stage, because it leaps to conclusions based on evidence that is (and must always logically remain) formally inadequate.

The "matters" of Perception and the Matter of enlightened thought belong in this sphere. It was Reason "operating as Understanding" that moved Consciousness from Perception to Understanding. But true Understanding achieves knowledge that is properly *a priori*, not the certainty that "all crows are black." The knowledge of Nature that can be mathematically schematized belongs to the Understanding proper. Rational knowledge must be intellectually schematized on the conceptual model of the self.

This discovery moves us to the higher level of Organic Observation. Here Reason in its "instinctive" phase requires the hypothesis of the "Author of Nature." This *Vorstellung* is simply the objective image of Reason as an end in itself. It transforms the true speculative Concept of Teleology (the Self-Concept, or the Concept that realizes itself) into External Teleology (the purpose realized in "matter" by a "mind"). *We* know that Reason is now observing itself, but it takes itself to be observing the "inner design" that is "behind the curtain." Its object is the living organism as an instinctively self-preservative and self-reproductive system. The observer knows that this is an "end in itself," but she feels obliged to assume that this rational aspect of the organism originates in the mind of a higher intelligence.

This rational end is present in the organism as a "soul." It reveals itself to the observing intelligence through the activity of the organic body. Hence the problem of Observation at this level is to construct the concept of the soul by employing the logical law of expressive identity: The observable variety of the organism's functioning and behaviour *expresses* the inward unity.

The totality of life in its environment refers us onwards to the organism as the living microcosm, the true end in itself, and the objective reality of Observing Reason. Even at the beginning of the discussion, we find Hegel stating the conclusion that can be reached logically only at the end: that there is not, and cannot be, an understandable *law* governing the interaction between the organism and its environment. The concept of the inorganic environment is what Reason has already constructed. So we can skip over the lengthy discussion of the "inner and outer" and the "inner and outer of the inner" (and finally of the "outer"). The same point—that no "law" is possible—is made over and over again. I shall explain what the terms mean and discuss briefly what leads Hegel to linger so long on this topic.

Generally, the "inner" is the soul and the "outer" is the body. The "inner of the inner" is the universal life-force flowing through all the forms of life (which we have already met as the "Infinite Life"). The "outer" of this "inner" is the actual life of the organism as a set of active functions: sensibility, irritability, and reproduction. On the side of the body, it is the materialized form of these functions as systems of organs (nerves for sensibility, muscles for irritability, etc.) that is the *physical* "inner" (being literally contained within the "outer" frame of the bony skeleton).

The reason Hegel belabours his points, emerges clearly when he begins to offer examples of the "formalist" philosophy of Nature (W. and C. 189:23–190:32; Miller ¶282). We can see from the Preface (W. and C. 37:3–39:18; Miller ¶¶50–52) that Hegel was deeply concerned about the rise of this sort of formalism in "Schelling's School." But we should not let this reason for prolixity blind us to the deeper truth that the whole philosophy of Nature as such is put into its cognitive place in this chapter. Behind the follies of the "formalists" there is the "critical" limitation upon the knowledge of Nature as such. Natural Science only leads us back to the Universal Life that is "indifferent to the kind of mills it drives" (W. and C. 191:31–33; Miller ¶285).

This is what we are forced to learn from the last movement of Natural Observation, when the organism is placed in its environment and the order of life itself on Earth is observed. There is a logical order of living species, distinguished in some way by *number*. But it is all broken and dislocated by the chancy character of the environment supplied by Earth (the "universal individual"). The relation of organism to environment (the "total" shapes of "inner and outer") is one of loose "influence." (As I see it, it is a simple matter to put our own evolutionary *Vorstellung* of life on Earth in the place of Hegel's non-evolutionary but chance-governed picture.)

3. Observation of the Self

When Life in its earthly environment is inverted from object of observation into subject of experience, we have nothing less than the World-Spirit before us. But for Observing Reason, this takes shape as the inversion of the vanishing life-force into the vanishing subject of pure speculative thinking. It is likely that Hegel would say that my reading of the Observation of Nature as a Kantian critical dismissal of the Philosophy of Nature is a mistake, because the real lesson of natural Life's "indifference to its mills" is that the meaning of Life is to be found in Self-Consciousness (and that of Nature in Spirit). But whichever way we look at it (critically or speculatively), the fact remains that this turning point in consciousness is a vanishing point. When Observing Reason tries to observe its own activity *as* Reason, it can find only the "laws of thought." These are without truth, because the logic of exclusive truth and falsity is an *ens rationis*. For us (or "in themselves" as principles of thinking), the logical principles are speculative "laws," because they *unite* the opposites (identity and contradiction) in a cyclic motion; but only the empty forms can be *found* by observation. The living motion of speculative logic lies just beyond the terminus of our experiential science.

The real self is a self-assertive practical agent. Logic is the *concept* of the self (which is not directly observable), and Psychology is its reality. Rational Observation aims to study the immediate reality of the singular subject, but the self-conscious rational agent exists (like the organism) in a universal context (the social world of Spirit, not the natural world of life). So Psychology has to deal with the educational relation between ethical life and the individual, and with her reciprocal action upon it. (Rational Psychology is a normative rather than an empirical science.)

Again Observation finds nothing but empty forms. The self is observed as a chance collection of "faculties, inclinations and passions." But a "law of individuality" can be stated which is the spiritual analogue of the organic law of expression. "Individuality" is the *result* of the motion that reintegrates Psychology into Logic. The three possible relations between self and world—simple reception, reformative reaction, and passive indifference—are all essential components in an active life; and the "law" is that of the Leibnizian *Monadology*: Every individual mirrors the world in her own way.

It is easy to overlook the importance of this "result." But anyone who has done biographical work (or read any that was well done) will appreciate the logical truth and insight of these few pages; and we shall soon recognize the continuing significance of the *Monadology* in our progress. Hegel *thaws* the frozen theological rationalism of Leibniz and shows it to us as a concept of actual experience.

Biography, however, is possible only in the case of the individual who is dead (or at least with respect to a life that is treated as complete). The psychologist needs a "law" that would make possible the prediction of the living individual's interaction with the world. This obliges us to consider the supposed "sciences" of Physiognomy and Phrenology. Nowadays, we are well aware that these curious disciplines were not, and could never become, sciences; but Hegel was one of the pioneers in saying this, and he was not generally heeded. Physiognomy had already a long history that began in Aristotle's school, and Phrenology (which was new) held on to a measure of scientific respect for a century after Hegel's time.

It must be conceded that here again Hegel is unduly prolix. We have to take our "result" and observe it as a subjective focus of life in action, and in this third phase of Observation we must necessarily return to the "Observation of Nature" in order to integrate it into our methodic progression. But the task could have been completed with the same brevity that was meted out to Logic and Psychology.

Lavater's Physiognomy purports to be the science of "body-language." It fails to become a science, first, because the expressive "speech" of the body cannot be turned into scientific language, and, secondly, because bodily expression is *essentially* subject to voluntary control. First, the scientific observer cannot record her data effectively. We might claim that the movie camera has overcome this difficulty, but the second one remains. Any "law" that is put forward can be falsified at will, once the subject knows what is claimed.

The way forward from bodily observation comes to our notice

incidentally, when Hegel points out that the self is what it does in the world (rather than what it secretly intends but does not do [W. and C. 212:36–38; Miller ¶319]); and the reason that Phrenology cannot be a science is also anticipated (W. and C. 209:14–23; Miller ¶314). Obviously, therefore, Hegel lingers with Phrenology only because the Science of Experience needs it.

When the living body proves not to be a viable means of access to the "inner" as what is "in itself" (precisely because the living body is the medium of transition from what is "in itself" to what is for everyone), all that is left for Observing Reason is the body as a being-in-itself. Can we discover from its outward appearance what the living consciousness is inwardly? The answer is obviously no, and the reason is simple. Even if we could identify where the record is, we could not read it. The necessary conventions for the interpretation of what is there are completely arbitrary, and they cannot be fixed.

Since Hegel carefully records Lavater's own use of this argument against Gall's Phrenology, it is clear that he wants us to see the transition from Physiognomy to Phrenology as the movement of the "self-conscious body" Concept into its direct antithesis, the dead body. This closes Observing Reason into a perfect circle, since at this stage the observer sees herself as a mere element in the Mineralogical Organism—which was phase one, the living Infinite of Nature.

The transition from the dead self-record to the active Spirit as a process of individual self-making is through the recognition of where the record really is; that is, in memory. The "infinite Judgement" that "the Self is a thing" is crucial to Hegel's experiential science, for it is at this point that we face *rationally* the inevitability of our own *natural* death. All of rational consciousness must lie in the grave and become a skull. But when we take the skull from the hands of the real F. J. Gall and give it to the imaginary Prince Hamlet, the miracle of resurrection happens. Instead of an absurd science, we have Yorick, that fellow of infinite jest and most excellent fancy, who gave the Prince his first lessons about life.

4. Active Reason

The modern Hamlet-self is actually the Faust of Goethe's 1790 Fragment. Faust turns his back on the "gray in gray" of scientific observation and seeks to pluck the fruit of "Life's golden tree." He will find the objective structure of the spiritual world, in which he lives and moves, to be a harsh impersonal Necessity; and the result of his encounter will be a conscious opposition between two Universal Laws (subjective and objective). This opposition evolves into identity, and finally the rational individual discovers that there is nothing left to fight against. At that point, we shall have reached the ordinary standpoint of enlightened common sense, which we regard as the *natural* attitude in our own social world.

The climax of the movement that begins here is the recovery of the Ethical Substance. So Hegel needs to introduce the Ethical Substance at the beginning, as the other side of the starting point, the *fulfilled* identity of Necessity with the immediate spiritual union of Faust and Gretchen in their love. The "Pleasure" of which Hegel speaks is not that of an ordinary selfish hedonist, for that is not "rational" at all. "Pleasure" is the spiritual identity of oneself with another which rises out of the natural sexual connection; the mutual enjoyment of Faust and Gretchen is the universal *world* of their love-relationship. It is that family bond which Hegel will later call the "element" of the Ethical Substance. Faust is selfish, and he smashes the little world of personal happiness "with mighty fist [*Faust*]" (as the Mephistophelean spirits foretell). But as we see the disaster from the inside, the happiness of the two lovers is smashed upon the harsh Necessity of social convention.

Gretchen, as she goes home from the scene "At the Well" meditating on her own "night of love," and on the social disgrace of another girl, is already discovering the next step in the dialectical progression. The social world itself ought to be governed by the "Law of the Heart," the law of universal love. The best model for this *Gestalt* seems to be the Savoyard Vicar in Rousseau's *Émile*. The Heart-Law seeks to sublate the cruelty of Necessity by means of devotion to the universal welfare of humanity. The Heart's "pleasure" is to love its fellows universally. But this "law," when proclaimed, is as much of an imposition on all other hearts as the harsh rule of Necessity was. So the Heart is driven to the *mad* hypothesis that its own law is not spontaneously received and obeyed because the rest of the world has been deluded by a corrupt system of government.

The *Gestalt* of this Frenzy of Self-Conceit is clearly Karl Moor, in Schiller's *The Robbers*. He becomes a brigand-leader with the goals typically ascribed to Robin Hood. In the play, however, he moves to the position that *results* from this inversion of the Heart's Law.

He dies a convert to the gospel of "Virtue." The "knight of virtue" has understood that the social order is necessary, and he wants to show us all that unselfish devotion to the public good is the secret of rational happiness.

The model of this *virtuous* attitude is certainly *not* Don Quixote (who belongs to an earlier world and could not represent the world of Reason). This unfortunate suggestion by Josiah Royce—which he half withdrew himself—has seriously distorted the interpretation of the section in many discussions. When we reflect that the political freedom of the community is perhaps the only form of the "public good" to which individuals can be quite *unselfishly* devoted, we can see that the right model is someone like Marquis Posa (in Schiller's *Don Carlos*). In the development of the *Gestalt*, the virtuous knight finds himself quite helpless in his opposition to the ordinary self-interested maintenance of the social order. Virtue is faced by the "Way of the World," and the motto of the World's Way can be expressed in the phrase "honesty is the best policy." But whatever is "honest" the knight of Virtue cannot touch. He must even be respectful of everything good that is produced by vicious motives. So Virtue ends up by collapsing into identity with the World's Way. This does have the significant "result" that the World learns that its own honesty is itself "public-spirited." The recognized identity of the public interest with the private good (of Faustian "happiness") is the completion of the *Bildung* of "real Individuality."

The shapes of Self-Actualizing Reason are often treated as "forms of individualism," but that is not how they are meant. Faust is certainly an "individualist," but we cannot understand even his role here, if we look at it in that light. What we are observing is the evolution of the concept of *society* in the mind of the individual who begins by regarding it as simply irrelevant. We begin and end with "forms of individualism," but in the end the individual has recognized that she must be comfortably at home in society and genuinely devoted to its maintenance.

5. The Spiritual Animal Kingdom

When we reach the stable society of the Real Individuals, we can recognize at once that we have finally arrived at the critical level from which Hegel's fifth chapter began. Hegel himself tells us that

Reason is now *conscious* (not "instinctive") idealism. The "self" in which community and individual are mutually identified is the Fichtean *Category* of the Ego. Reason's "Certainty" has coincided with its "Truth." All of the shapes of Reason (but not, for example, the shape of serfdom or of Unhappy Consciousness) *return* into this final society of equal recognition.

The *action* of these rational individuals simply manifests their natures; it changes nothing in the shared categorical structures of their world. What is manifested is the monadology of Reason that we met in the "law of individuality." This truth emerges gradually. The community that we have reached is what Hegel calls "Civil Society" in the *Philosophy of Right*, and it is natural to approach Civil Society with *economic* categories in mind. If we apply Hegel's metaphor of the "Spiritual Animal Kingdom" to this community, all the crafts and professions offer themselves readily to the mind as the "spiritual kinds." But the economic interpretation is misleading, because it places too much emphasis on material prosperity. The *Sache selbst*, the universal result of this stage, is not *money* (or commodities), though that is arguably *one* of its outward aspects. The whole conception of spiritual *kinds* involves classification by external comparison; and eventually Hegel rules this out decisively (W. and C. 265:27–266:35; Miller ¶¶403–404). Every rational individual (like the angels of Aquinas) is her own unique species, and the universal medium of manifestation is her *speech*. The *Sache selbst* of this spiritual kingdom is the concept of Social Utility maintained in linguistic communication. (But the reading of the Spiritual Animal Kingdom as the community of professors and artists is more misguided than the simple economic interpretation, because it is not a properly *universal* community; all of us in the World of Reason are Real Individuals.)

The spiritual animals all maintain their devotion to the public good, but their behaviour in relation to this *realized Sache selbst* reveals the hypocrisy of their position. Their Virtue (now called *Ehrlichkeit*, or Worthiness) is only a cloak for the World's Way, and by exposing to view the appropriate moment of the categorical *Sache selbst*, they can demonstrate the worthiness of supposed social contributions that are no more than verbal self-approbation for doing nothing. In the case of *real* contributions, the impossibility of eliminating the aspect of *individual* self-realization in any *specific* activity drives us to recognize that only the speaker who seeks to make laws for the community can succeed in expressing the *Sache selbst* purely.

In the dialectical motion of the Spiritual Animal Kingdom, the *Sache selbst* (of worthiness or social utility) is first inverted directly into hypocritical pretence, and then the comprehensive second inversion of the two poles together produces the concrete individuality of Reason. The rational individual identifies with the ideal substance of the community (i.e., with its *law*), so that the whole problem of individual self-realization is sublated. The *Sache selbst* ceases to be a predicate of the "work" produced and becomes the subject itself.

6. Law-Giving and Law-Testing

The lawgiver was a familiar figure in the tradition of the Ethical Substance, but he did not make laws by simply using his unaided subjective Reason. He began with the customs and institutions that already existed, and remodelled them in order to resolve the problems that had made his intervention necessary. The situation of Individual Reason as lawgiver is radically different, because that social substance has been forgotten. But the substance is still *there*, and the fully developed individual Reason will not turn against it (as Faust did). The difficulty is that it does not understand its own role in relation to the substance; and in trying to generate it as a whole out of nothing, so to speak, the individual can produce only the most elementary and general statements of principle. These fall far short of being laws that can be applied unambiguously to actual cases.

Hegel discusses two examples: one that was fundamental to the Ethical Substance as it arose naturally (and which remains fundamental in all phases of its development); and one that points to the ultimate goal of the *morally* Ethical Substance which is now coming into existence (and which remains always a regulative ideal that is beyond adequate concrete embodiment). As principles of rational common sense, both of the exemplars are essentially dialectical. First comes "Tell the truth," and then "Love thy neighbour."

"Tell the truth" is an impossible commandment (when taken *absolutely*) because we must *know* the truth in order to express it. *This* is the ultimate imperative of our existence (and we *can* satisfy it in the philosophical sense, as we shall see), but empirically we can only tell the truth according to what we know (or believe). The law does not command this, so the law lies. This criticism is sophistical, because it is easy enough to state the law with its appropriate qualification. When we do that, it becomes the familiar guide of our lives, but it will not lead us towards deeper insight into what "the truth" absolutely *is*.

"Love thy neighbour." This means "Do what is good for her." But to do that I must *know* what is good; and even if I know what is *contingently* good in given circumstances, this should not blind me to the fact that I can do *no* good for my neighbour (or myself) unless we are participants in the great common good that we call "the State." It is our commitment to, and membership in, the community—that is, a *human* community consciously directed towards the good life—that enables us to be good to one another (insofar as we can) in our contingent ways.

Thus, the Ethical Substance has now appeared to us. It only remains for us to examine the function of our critical Reason in relation to it. Can we tell formally what is a *good* law and what is not? By simple observation we cannot do this. Critical observation is what we are doing ourselves; but we are not trying to *test* anything. We are only watching the absolute truth evolve by testing itself.

Hegel's claim that Law-testing Reason is only the empty standard of formal consistency must be understood in the light of this identity with our own standpoint. The formal consistency of Critical Reason is not the formal tautology of the "Laws of Thought." We *do* know what a "just law" is, and that is an essential *moment* in the existence and evolution of the Ethical Substance. But it is insufficient for the generation of a system of justice.

The fact that we cannot decide by using pure Reason whether property should be held privately or communally reflects the fact that all property (as the medium of rational action) is both private and communal; and from that consequence of the finitude of individual Reason springs the dialectical character of justice. The concept of property *emerges* naturally through the self-assertion of singular Self-Consciousness. But the concept of Justice as "giving to each her due" which this generates proves to be a dialectical contradiction as soon as the principle of "loving our neighbour" is applied to it. For in that perspective, we can see that what is "due" to each individual is not simply the "telling of truth and payment of debts" but the best possible opportunity to realize herself and to contribute to the common good. We can never achieve both of these requirements at once; so it is a necessary truth that the just society is unjust.

This is an incidental reflection on the reason why the Ethical Substance must always continue to spin upon its axis. The axis itself, we can now see, is to be found in the "instinct of Reason"— that is, in its natural embodiment. We must listen to the voice of Nature that gave Antigone her "unwritten laws." There cannot *be* Justice at all—because there cannot be any rationally universal consciousness—if the natural origins of the spiritual consciousness that overcomes our natural finitude are ignored or violated. Reason as the test of laws *does* become critically necessary eventually, because it is the "natural" Law itself (as what primitively *is*) that develops into the critical Reason of the individual. But that is the theme of the next chapter.

Chapter 7
Spirit

1. Finite and Absolute Spirit

By now, it should be obvious that there is nothing mysterious (or mystical) about Hegel's concept of Spirit. Wherever two or more individuals can talk to one another successfully about some good of a non-instrumental kind that they have (or can hope to have) in common, there the Spirit exists. We all know that we are not *born* rational, that we must *learn* to talk, and that it is only through education that we discover that there are goods other than the satisfaction (or satiation) of natural bodily desires and needs. This education is the genesis of the Spirit for us (and of our truly *human* selves in the Spirit that we recognize as already existing).

But the *objective* concept of Spirit that we have now reached is more than the control of language in our conversation with parents and teachers. We already know that the *real* Spirit that exists and demands our recognition is "the State;" in other words, it is the developed political community that maintains the school, and a great complex of other institutions which require our service and which protect or facilitate our free self-expression in a variety of ways. It is the development of this political community, from the logical point of origin that we have just now identified, which we shall now observe.

Spirit is the unity of our world as we are conscious of it. This ⟍ functional definition will be adequate even for Absolute Spirit, which is the unity of our natural and our (objectively) spiritual world. Typically, we project the Absolute Spirit as "another self" (or a community of selves), which we call "God" (or "the Gods"). This is necessary because we cannot successfully comprehend the unity of our world of objective Spirit—in the ordinary commonsensical mode of "Consciousness"—without making this kind of projection. But if we can conceptualize the objective Spirit successfully—that is to say, overcome the apparent otherness of the community as "another self" in our *Vorstellung*—then we shall not find that the *absolute* otherness of Absolute Spirit poses any insuperable problem for us. The key to the solution of these problems is the methodically cumulative comprehension of our experience.

All of the "shapes" of the singular consciousness that we have so far observed are only moments that have their being within the objective totality of our institutionalized life. We can understand this claim readily enough simply by considering the education process through which we have ourselves been "spiritualized." We may think of Sense-Certainty as belonging to us privately, but it already refers us to a world of real Things with names that we did not give them; and the world of Perception is quite evidently a social construct. The shapes of Self-Consciousness teach us how important the substantial preservation of the temporal record is. Spirit *exists* most vividly in memory, and Objective Spirit is the organized preservation of social memory (or "tradition").

2. "True" Spirit

It is easy to characterize Objective Spirit *as* an "object," but how does it become the "subject" of experience (as it has to at this point)? The answer is simple. It becomes "subject" as the self-conscious "absolute" knowledge of every member of the community. Unlike Saint Joan, Antigone does not claim to "hear voices," but she *knows* absolutely what the laws of her supreme God are. More generally (and less dramatically), everyone knows what the customary way of life of their community requires. It is the task of their poets to represent for them clearly the *absoluteness*—the inviolable sacredness—of this common way. This is the common substance of their accidental mortal existences. They do not—indeed, they *must not*—argue about it or criticize it. They become objectively aware of it (as an eternal essence) through its artistic portrayal. Hence, it is that portrayal that we must observe.

The world of this True Spirit (in which all fully rational individuals identify directly with the absolute knowledge of their common substance as the "Truth" of their mortal being) is a nation (the Hellenes) divided naturally by geography into tribal "masses." Each of these "masses" has built up its own set of laws and customs on the basis of a set of customs and traditions that are common to all who use the Greek language. The "masses" are aggressive; they fight one another to establish and express their "freedom" (i.e., the independence and autonomy of their own humanly made "constitutions)."

For this reason, they are naturally led to segregate their womenfolk and to keep them out of men's affairs. The making and running of their own "constitution" becomes an exclusively male preserve. Nobody *decides* this; it just happens, and it happens everywhere. Thus, it is part of the "Divine Law"—the body of customs shared by all of the particular communities. For this reason, (and also because of their naturally determined function as *mothers*), the womenfolk are ethically bound to regard their own particular community—their *polis*—under its natural aspect (or as a mass of *families*). This is what the mass already was before it became a politically constituted community, so what the womenfolk know *absolutely* is the "Divine Law"—the customs whose establishment is beyond all conscious memory, and which the other communities all share. The menfolk, in contrast, are devoted to the customs that they know to be peculiarly theirs, the things for which they must fight and die; and one of the most important of these is the life-and-death authority of their leader.

The "Cities" in this Hellenic community will not normally have to fight about the sacredness of a "divine" custom, because it is equally sacred for all of them. And there will not normally be conflicts between the Divine and the Human Law within the City, because every City must cultivate and institutionalize the "divine" customs in order to maintain the devotion of its warriors. It is bound, in particular, to have a human law of legitimate marriage, because "membership" and the duty of absolute commitment must be clearly recognized; and if anyone betrays his duty to the City, he must (at least) be excluded from the community.

How far should such exclusion go? That is not very obvious. But the myth of two royal brothers who fell into a prepolitical feud about the "kingship" offered Sophocles a perfect occasion to dramatize the answer clearly. A declared traitor may be banished, and even when dead he may be dishonoured. But his body should be surrendered to his family for burial. Even dead enemies from other Cities must be buried properly.

The *Antigone*, in which this truth is shown, also dramatizes the proper relation of the men and women within Substance.

Antigone's sister Ismene declares at the outset that the woman's part is to leave political affairs to the men even if the Divine Law is violated. But Antigone acts politically and violates Creon's edict in order to bury her brother Polyneices. Thus, there occurs a tragic collision between the two laws. Both of the protagonists assert the "absolute right of Self-Consciousness" against the "divine right of the Substance," and each is quite right in accusing the other of doing this. Antigone says that Creon is a tyrant, and he says that she is an outrageously self-willed young hussy. The play shows (through the eventual intervention of Tiresias) that this clash of self-wills was quite unnecessary, and the guilty parties suffer equal penalties (as Antigone herself prophesies).

Hegel's analysis of the Ethical Substance contains some factual mistakes, but he is right about the emergence of the self-conscious singular will as the only source of law. Among his errors we must count the claim that "woman presides" over the Family and the Divine Law (W. and C. 301:4–6; Miller ¶459). This mistake seems to be connected with the later claim that "the community . . . creates in womankind its own inner enemy" (W. and C. 314:1–6; Miller ¶475); that claim itself is true only *mythically* (i.e., where "womankind" means simply "the Family"). Alternatively, we can say that it was true about the male image of woman; but there is no intelligible sense in which the womenfolk of Hellas destroyed its political system.

Hegel's most interesting error was his attempt to interpret Antigone's essentially sophistical argument that she had a special duty to her dead brother because he was irreplaceable as a "truth" of the Ethical Substance. He deserves credit for resisting Goethe's foolish argument that the sophistry of this speech is inconsistent with Antigone's character as a martyr of conscience, for he is quite right that she is not a martyr of conscience at all. But the unique importance of the brother-sister relation belongs only to the "returned" community of Absolute Spirit (in which, to quote the Saviour, "there is neither marrying nor giving in marriage"), and not to Greek ethics at all. The tortured relations of Hegel and his sister are philosophically quite irrelevant. But we should note that his willing acceptance of Antigone as a free individual agent on a par with Creon has revolutionary implications for his later attempt to portray her ideal of the woman's lot as the final truth of the modern political community. *We* can no longer see Antigone in the way that Sophocles saw her, precisely because these implications have fully declared themselves in our world, and we accept them as "true." Antigone did not *want* to be a political agent; but that is what she shows herself—and all her sisters—to be.

3. The Condition of Right

The equality of Antigone and Creon as self-assertive free agents who express the "absolute right of Self-Consciousness" without meaning to do anything of the sort is essential to the transition that we must now make to the world of legal individuals. In True Spirit, the equal recognition of individuality is entirely spiritual. Only those who have paid the debt of death to the Substance can be recognized as free individuals. But when the empire builders came (beginning with Alexander, but triumphing finally only with Augustus) the community of True Spirit perished, because the Cities were no longer free and "self-sufficient."

All communities were now subject to a law that took no account of them as abiding substances, but recognized only their mortal members. The resulting universal community was "spiritless" because there was no *living* bond between the mortals and the *truth* of their lives. The legal theorists of the world pacified by Roman Law were philosophically Stoics, but their God was only a formal abstraction. The real world was cut off from any absolute truth; Legal Right was the *actual* realization of Scepticism (just as Scepticism was the *conceptual* realization of Stoicism). Everyone was legally constituted as a completely independent *essence*, but there were only finite essences in the picture. The real "Lord of the World" is not the Stoic God of Reason and Nature, but a mortal living man who becomes a God when he dies.

Every time death asserts *its* lordship, the whole system is in peril, for now it becomes explicit that the *absolute* law is "the law of the stronger." Anarchy reigns, and the world goes mad. The system is supposed to keep the legalized world safe from the "barbarians" beyond its frontier, but the raging of the rival armies inside the Empire is the same tumult of natural passions that exists outside it. Authority is maintained only by appalling savagery. When Hegel speaks of "monstrous excess" and the "casting away of self-consciousness" (W. and C. 310:11 and 33; Miller ¶¶481–482), we should think of military tyrants like Caracalla, rather than of ac-

tual madmen like Caligula and Elagabalus. For it is the *world*-mad-
ness represented by the execution of a great lawyer like Papinian
that Hegel means us to remember.

It is quite impossible for the rational self to recognize itself in
Caracalla. The Gods (all organized into a Pantheon of legal recognition) have left the world, so the *result* of the actualization of
Stoicism as Scepticism is the emergence of the Unhappy Consciousness. In the "first relation" of the world (to God as Judge),
"the Lord" is not Yahweh but simply *Death*. In the realm of "the
Unchangeable" there is nothing but death to be seen. Only with
the Conversion of Constantine will the "second relationship"
begin.

4. Spirit in Self-Estrangement

The next stage in the evolution of Spirit corresponds both to the
Unhappy Consciousness and to Instinctive Reason in the logic of
the singular self. It takes us all the way from Constantine to the
Revolution of 1789. But the order of the logical moments is not
strictly historical. First, we have to follow the realization of Faith
in the actual world and its transformation into Insight on the very
verge of the Revolution; then we can comprehend the exposition
of the estranged Concept as a concept and the story of its universalization as Enlightenment; and, finally, we observe the actualization of Enlightenment in the Revolution itself. We go round the
circle twice, and that is appropriate because Consciousness is itself
doubled (or self-estranged).

In the Roman Empire, Bondage was universalized. There was
a Universal Lord on Earth in the shape of the Emperor, but in the
world beyond, Death was the only universal destiny. When the
Christian Gospel took the place of the Imperial Cult, the world
beyond became the real world of Thought. That was God's place,
and the finite consciousness in this world was estranged from its
true *essence*. This is the condition of *Faith*. What we *know* does not
verify itself in our experience; knowledge of the truth is *postponed*.

But as the experience of an actual world, the life of Faith is *objective* in a way that Unhappy Consciousness was not. "Culture" is
the *reforming* of the natural self into a new spiritual self, and this
involves the reforming of the social world out of its "atoms and

void" condition into a properly spiritual community of shared values. This is quite *visible* to Faith, so Faith is the "third relation" of the Unhappy Consciousness (as distinct from the "second relation," which we have already observed). The equality of recognition in this new world is not that of equality before the law, but that of brothers and sisters in the sight of God; but this spiritual equality is *estranged*, since the actual world is a mass of social differences.

The value-system of universal Culture develops from the stark alternatives of Salvation (Good) and Damnation (Bad). The first choice that faces us is that between the religious and the secular life. But since Faith holds that we can *all* be saved, this simple Judgement is not enough. In the world of Culture there are *four* masses (in place of the *two* laws of the Ethical Substance). The Community as Church Militant is saved in the "Air" of the Spirit; as the Civil Society of the Spiritual Animal Kingdom (itself divided into four sub-masses: the peasantry and the three recognized Estates of the Ancien Régime), the community is the Water of the Spirit; as Universal Enlightenment, it will become the Fire in which all is consumed; and as the national Economy, it is the Earth of Spirit (see W. and C. 326:21–328:25; Miller ¶¶492–494). The Air of Faith and the Fire of Enlightenment enter in place of the Divine Law; the Earth of Natural Life and the Water of Culture enter in place of the Human Law. Air and Earth are Good and Bad *simply*, but in the social structure of the estranged world these "pure thoughts" become the real goals of actual existence. The Good is the public service, and the Bad is the quest for Wealth. But it is perfectly possible to choose either, both, or neither, with the intent of achieving salvation.

Let us consider mixed choices first. On the one side, the bourgeois private citizen sets happiness as the goal of life in the shape of family prosperity (Wealth), but she accepts the maintenance of the State Power as the necessary instrumental condition of all such prosperity. On the other side, the salaried civil servant makes a choice that has the opposite structure. These two "mixed" judgements are important to society but not to us, because they are not made "absolutely."

The interesting choices are the one that takes both State Power and Wealth as Good and that which takes them both to be Bad. The first is the choice of the Noble Mind. Here, the State Power is iden-

tified as the Good, but Wealth pertains to the singular self naturally, because the Noble has a family estate. On the other side, the
"contemptuous" consciousness (which is *not* "base," and certainly
not "base-born") despises both the goals of the actual world. This
choice is made by the clergy (at the beginning of our story) and by
enlightened Insight (at the end), but it is the choice of Insight that
matters to us.

The main movement of the section deals with the transformation of Noble-mindedness into Enlightened Contempt. This is a
"syllogism" through which the opposite "Judgements" of Culture
are connected. We begin with the Noble consciousness as a *mute*
service of the State Power. This is the ideal of *Knighthood*, and this
undeveloped Concept already contains "Contempt" as its own
inner antithesis. The simple Knight must have a Lord from whom
he receives his life-support. But the Lord is himself a knight; and in
his service to the State Power, he can become a "haughty vassal" of
his Lord. This higher lord is the King, who is generally *identified*
with the State Power, but only symbolically, not yet as its acknowl-
edged "self-consciousness." All of the King's barons are his
"peers" in their service to the State Power; so rebellious "contempt" is quite justifiable in their minds. The "counsel" that they
pretend to give to the King may turn into revolt. It is only with
their swords that they speak unambiguously.

This mute ambiguity is overcome when, through a new kind of
speech, the barons constitute the Monarch as "absolute." Louis
XIV can say, "I am the State," because the whole ruling class con-
firms this. The change is effective because both the distribution of
honour and the control of Wealth passes into the King's hands.
Noble-mindedness dissociates both itself and the State Power into
the two sides of "public Good" and "pure self-will." All selfhood
is surrendered to the Monarch in speech, and in return the Monarch distributes the public Good (in the shape of salaried offices
under the Crown). What was originally the heroism of service becomes the heroism of flattery. The nobles surrender their rational
selfhood in return for their "privileges," and the Monarch becomes
their agent and universal servant.

Because the system of the Absolute Monarchy is a system of
irrational privilege, it deserves "Contempt." The Nobles are no
longer noble-minded. They are grateful only to their Royal benefactor, and arrogantly contemptuous of everyone else. There is no

distinction between the Nobility and the bourgeoisie. Anyone who has enough wealth (from any source) can be a "benefactor." So the completely Contemptuous consciousness is that of Rameau's Nephew, who is a cynical client of the bourgeois rich. He has returned to the ideal of Noble-mindedness at the higher level of conscious speech. But his language of Absolute Culture is a mass of contradictions, because he exists at two levels. As the rational consciousness of human dignity and freedom he is noble, but as the consciousness of the universality of self-seeking he can only be contemptuous of all actual consciousness, including especially himself. In this world of unearned privilege, all values are corrupt and the hypocrisy of all "worthies" is patent.

5. Faith and Pure Insight ∠

Young Rameau does not know how to escape from his predicament, but Diderot (whom Hegel wrongly took to be his creator rather than his chronicler) has grasped that the true nobility of humanity is in the higher realm of pure thought. Thus, what happens now is a move from the world of actuality to that of thought. Young Rameau's "other world" of Faith (which was with us all through "Culture") is simply the "other side" of our consciousness of the actual world. But now, in its naive form as an other world of *existence*, it has emerged as the internal opposite of Insight itself: The "Kingdom of Heaven" is just the *thought* of a life-world set free from contradiction. But Faith knows that this Kingdom is *substantial*; it has crossed the threshold where the Unhappy Consciousness came to a reverent halt. All of its labour in the world of Culture has been for the sake of "Kingdom Come." So it cannot lightly surrender its existential consciousness of the thought-world; it is an aspect of Insight (which thus becomes the practical project of a world founded upon the universal recognition of human dignity). Faith and Insight must remain locked in conflict until they emerge united as the "rational faith" of Moral Reason.

In Hegel's account of the content of Faith, we can already see the seed of the Manifest Religion that will be born from the completed evolution of "rational faith." The world of Faith is simply the dogma of the Trinity transformed into abstract concepts. Abstraction is the form of existential estrangement. God, in his Kingdom, reveals himself to us by stages, and this revelation is actually his unalienated identity with us in the one true world of the Spirit. Our world is "fallen," but we must bring it back to him—and we can do that because he is present to us inwardly *now*, "in the Spirit." In this aspect, we can readily identify Faith as the "third relation" of the Unhappy Consciousness. It experiences its salvation as the inner side of its actual life (cf. W. and C. 146:1–4; Miller ¶210).

This Faith is the *object* of Pure Insight. Insight is the self-actualizing power of the Concept for which Faith is the content. It seeks first to turn both of the modes of independent being (both the cultured world and the world of Faith) into pure concepts. But it is only a *project* when it appears—a singular experience that must become universal. The shattered consciousness of Young Rameau's world must be reconciled and reintegrated. In its universalized shape, Insight is the Enlightenment, and Rameau becomes only a necessary moment.

6. The Enlightenment

The concept of Insight was the *result* of the motion of Culture. The Enlightenment displays the *experience* of this Concept. This experience is the evolution of a different kind of *Bildung*, in which the pure concept formed in the actual world turns around to reform actuality. Logically, this experience only completes the parallel between the exposition of Insight and that of Faith. The actualization of Enlightenment itself has two sides: There is a great flurry in the daylight of consciousness—typified by *Rameau's Nephew*—and behind that a silent transformation of Faith into Enlightenment (which is irresistible because it is already complete by the time it becomes fully conscious).

Enlightenment is a "struggle with superstition" because Faith appears to it as an *impure* form of itself. Faith is *used* by the authorities in the actual world to support a completely irrational system of privilege. Insight proper must avoid actual conflict (in which it would be merely a partisan); its task is to develop the natural Reason and love of honour in "the mass" (as it turns the Air of Faith into Fire).

The hero of this Struggle is Baron d'Holbach. He was, of course, a notorious atheist, but it is not in that character that he first ap-

pears. The Enlightenment had its *religious* side, and we must remember that, even among the Materialists, Helvétius preached a
sort of religious humanism. It is the "religion of humanity" that
best represents Insight.

The characterization of Faith as "superstition" is unjust and
sophistical. Insight takes everything that Faith says and does literally, whereas Faith knows that its truth is all inward. Hence
Faith can mount a counterattack against Insight; this is necessary
because the inward content of Faith must become the content of
Insight itself. Insight says that the God of Faith is a *projected fiction*; what is true is that he is the projected shape of Reason itself,
the universal Reason whose existence is Enlightenment's own
truth. Insight holds that Faith accepts the miracle of salvation on
the basis of historical testimony, but when Faith reads the testi-
monies it only accepts the inner witness of the Spirit. Insight
thinks that fasting and almsgiving, being at best only symbolic,
are absurd, but as a result, it falls back into contemplative hypocrisy itself.

Enlightenment does have its own positive truth. This is the finite truth of the empiricist philosophy from Locke to Reid. We
know only our own "ideas," and God is an *empty* concept. All actual cognition is singular, and what are known are the Things of
Sense-Certainty. This world of Things exists as the repertory of
rational utilities. Everything is just what it is for Reason. But the
real Things in Reason's world are the embodied rational selves,
who all make use of one another, so the world of Utility is the
sphere of reciprocal usefulness. This gospel of finite happiness is
an abomination to Faith, but it triumphs irresistibly.

Enlightenment only brings out the thoughtless contradictori-
ness of Faith. The absolute right of Self-Consciousness triumphs
once more over the divine right of the Substance. The negative
criticism is one-sided, but the external side of Faith that is attacked
is really there. So Faith is properly convicted of contradiction, and
it is the positive side of Enlightenment that survives in triumph.
Of course, Enlightenment does not recognize the substantial truth
of Faith, so its triumph will be short-lived. But at the end of the
"battle," all the thought-furniture of Faith has been restored to this
world. Faith can only mourn for what it has lost, and Enlightenment will now rid itself of this one remaining blemish on its finite
happiness.

7. The Truth of Enlightenment

The section in which the "blemish" is removed in principle looks
very like a simple repetition of the "positive side" of Enlightenment in the previous section. But Hegel would never present a
mere repetition as a new movement of thought. Logically, the
"Truth of Enlightenment" has to be the establishment of its validity as absolute knowledge; it is "pure metaphysics." But also, as a
phenomenological movement, it must be the transition from
thought back to actuality. Insight is now concerned with its own
existence in the world.

The first thing that happens is a novel development. The trium-
phant Enlightenment splits into its two sides; its absolute Truth is
the contradiction between Pure Thought and Pure Matter, or Deism and Materialism. But these opposites are such pure abstrac-
tions that their opposition is empty. When we grasp them together
as the sides of a unified concept, we have the abstract concept of
Utility; and Utility as it is grasped by the enlightened mind is a
"bad infinite" continuum of means and ends.

Hegel says that Utility may look bad to Faith, but it is the *realization* of Pure Insight. We are in the world of Rational Individuals,
but that world is not comprehended as the reality of the Self; it is
only the instrument. Therefore, a collision between the self and its
world becomes inevitable. On the side of the actual world, Culture
culminated in absolute *vanity*. Now the concept of Self-Culture
has absorbed Faith and realized Insight (as Deism/Materialism
and finite Utility). The Spiritual Animals have all vanished into
the rational equality of man as citizen. We are in a position to create Heaven on Earth—or so it seems. The estrangement between
actuality and thought appears to be completely overcome. What is
thought about now is the actual world. But the opposition between
thought and things (which is the form of estrangement involved in
Pure Insight) remains absolute; and the "useful things" are really
the self-assertive thinkers themselves.

8. Absolute Freedom and Terror

What is actualized in this *immediate* reconciliation of Spirit with
Nature is "Absolute Freedom." The rationally universal self is now
free (like the singular natural self at the beginning of our logical

story) to "do as it likes." But since it *is* rational, this freedom inheres in its *communal* activity. It is the Nation of free citizens that has emerged.

The emergence of the free Nation took place in France between 1789 and 1792. In this short period, we can clearly observe the liquidation both of the older "noble" status system of Culture and of the "Spiritual Animal Kingdom" established by Reason in transition. With the advent of the National Convention (elected by universal male suffrage), the moment arrives when all singular wills are direct participants in the General Will, and the Constitution thus established is the Will of All (in the speculative sense that *everyone* is rationally committed to its maintenance, not in the degenerate empirical sense that Rousseau gave to this expression). It is this "Will of All" that is "Absolute Freedom."

This sovereign freedom assumes the throne of the World on 22 September 1792 (with the abolition of the Monarchy and the establishment of the Republican Calendar). But already the newborn Nation is "in danger," and (instead of producing the sense of substantial "identity") the national danger brings out the contradiction between the universal and singular sides of "Absolute Freedom." Every citizen *is* the Nation incarnate, and the God of Deism is just a bad smell lingering over the corpse of the old Constitution.

The contradiction ought to be mediated by the *particularization* of individual freedom in a constitutional structure founded on the "Spiritual Animal Kingdom" (the status system of Culture has liquidated itself logically). But this task has to wait for Napoleon; it does not concern our Science, which needs only the crisis of the Terror in order to uncover the necessary *moral* basis of the new political order (in the principle of universal respect for individual dignity). This next step is easy to comprehend. Where every rational being *is* immediately the Universal, all have the same right to exercise absolute Freedom. Hence there is bound to be a "war of all against all," and not even those who would submit readily in the *natural* struggle can now be given any quarter. All are rational, so all are "suspect" (of perverting rationality into selfish ambition). Since the actual government is necessarily a tyrannically perverse *faction*, the suspicion is bound to be justified wherever it arises. The war must go on until its absurdity is recognized and the effective tyrants have themselves ridden in the last carts to the guillotine.

9. The Moral Worldview and Its Displacement

Faced with the guillotine, the enlightened rational consciousness is forced to recognize that its absolute Freedom exists in the realm of thought, not in that of actuality. We have arrived at the level of Rational Faith, and with the resolution of this antithesis we shall finally achieve the standpoint of Absolute Spirit.

The "intuition" of the Moral World is contained in the rational postulates identified in Kant's *Critique of Practical Reason*. Hegel organizes and states them in the logical order and shape that their effective dissolution requires. But that is only our legitimate "contribution." The basic contradiction that we have to recognize is that human moral freedom *from* Nature entails the equal freedom *of* Nature (as a living system). Consequently, the concept of "moral life" must be effectively estranged from its experience. We cannot enjoy the happiness of knowing that our duty is done and our moral vocation is realized. The harmony of moral action and moral satisfaction is empirically uncertain, but I must *postulate* it as a certainty. This postulate can be put off to the end of an "infinite progress"; indeed, it must be so interpreted, for if its fulfilment arrived, the dissatisfaction that occasions the experience of moral freedom would cease to exist. Therefore, I must transcend this "bad infinite" standpoint and postulate God as the ground of the harmony between nature and morality. But now I am in a position analogous to that of the Unhappy Consciousness. If *absolute* knowledge belongs to God, then I do not know whether I am a *moral* consciousness or not. I can look for felicity only as a gift of grace, and grace must be proportioned to my disposition, not my action. All truth is hidden in the supersensible world.

If we regard this *result* as our new conceptual subject, we have Fichte's Moral World Order. Hegel does not treat this as a logical advance, but only as another way of viewing the same position. Here the dialectic is clearer and simpler, because we can begin with the confident assumption that the finite consciousness *is* moral and proceed to show that it cannot be so; a morally *complete* self-consciousness does not exist, and therefore there is nothing morally actual. The actual unity of the moral self is only what *ought* to be: it is a *Sollen*. What Kant presents in the mode of Faith Fichte translates into the mode of Insight.

I have given only a very simplified account of the dialectic of the Moral Worldview, but it must be repeated now at the stage of "Displacement" (in which the "Certainty" of the Moral Sense becomes "Moral Perception." The whole of this section is produced by the logical operation of our own observing reason, so it is only methodically justified, because the motion was visible already at the "intuitive" level.

The difficulties of moral consciousness are overcome by postulating a world that belongs to God as the absolute Self. "Displacement" overthrows this equilibrated Concept and leads us to Conscience as the stable concept of the finitely absolute moral consciousness. "Rational Faith" is shown to be exactly what Freud called "rationalization"; it is a simple wish-fulfilment.

Kant's moral cosmology is "a nest of thoughtless contradictions" (as *he* said of the traditional Cosmological Argument). Consciousness jumps from position to position around a circle, without maintaining any of them seriously. The starting position is that there is actual moral consciousness in the natural world. But when the agent acts, the harmony is realized, so the postulate is not needed. Action is what matters.

One action, however, cannot make the harmony. Do we never really make progress? Nonsense, it is the doing of *duty* that matters, and that is a matter of *intent*, not of actual success. But this will not do, because it is the unity of the world-order that is important; and we cannot say that, because if it were achieved, action would be superfluous.

Perfection must be given up, because morality would be lost in it; so it is the intermediate state of things that is vital. How then, can *progress* be possible? Moral duty is not a matter of degrees, anyway. Being serious about the intermediate state, therefore, is only being serious about our non-morality. We have come back to the first position in negated form. We are not actually moral, so how can we make a rational demand for moral happiness? We can only hope to receive it by grace, and it is certainly immoral to hope for what is irrational.

But if *our* morality is *impure*, then the standard must be in God; my many duties are sanctified by God. No external power can make my duty holy, however, since no external power can be holy. The holy will supplies my own standard of duty as universal. But God cannot be the *perfect* moral consciousness, because, being above nature, he does not (and cannot) act. We must give him up.

But we see all of our contradictions united in him. The displacement has been between pure intention and actual performance as essential. But both of them are essential. They must be united in the self-certain Conscience.

10. Conscience and the Beautiful Soul

From the intuition of a world in Faith, we have come back to the self-certainty of Moral Reason. Conscience is the finite self that knows itself to be valid in all its contingency. That is to say, in spite of all the ways in which my knowledge is limited and my active choices are restricted, the conscientious awareness that "*this* is my duty" is categorically necessary (or absolutely "true"). Conscience is the final shape of the individual *person*. First, there was the legally recognized person, and then, as a result of the long discipline of Culture, we reached the citizen with the "natural rights" of universal Reason. Now we have the self-defining person with the right to absolute moral respect. This finite person is at the same time a *worldview*, because she is consciously *situated* in her actual social world. She is not even conceivable in abstraction from the legal and the rational selfhood that she sublates. ("Conscience" is *not* the self of the Heart's Law; we shall see *that* return only when Conscience breaks down.)

Conscience goes through the whole evolution of Consciousness. It begins as Moral Sense. The conscientious person follows an immediate conviction. Many duties may be abstractly conceivable, but I *know* what *my* duty is; however, since what I do is a public fact that can be interpreted in many ways, I must be able to explain what I do by *saying how* it is my duty. The harmony of universal recognition is the moral harmony that moral faith could not achieve; and as that harmony, Conscience is the fulfilled *Sache selbst*.

The *experience* of this Concept is to retreat into an ever narrower compass. Conscience does not move; it stands firm. Thus, it does not *know* everything, but it defines itself as the best that could be done with one's actual knowledge. Its certainty must come from *my* actual feelings, so it is necessarily capricious. I can think of it as my duty to get rich, or even to run away in a battle (because my wealth is that of the Nation and my life is socially useful). One is immoral only if one does not know what to say. (But if one commits an actual crime, one will not find oneself in the forum of Conscience; and if one does not do what is required by one's social *station*, one will suffer the normal penalties for that.) All of the deceitful shifts of the *Sache selbst* are available, and all external criticism remains irrelevant.

This pure knowledge of self is what has to be respected by all as what their own selfhood is; and if I accept some criticism, that only means that I have passed beyond the action of that earlier self and have become part of the critical audience. Criticism is always possible, because every action springs from some motive that is personal to me, but it is silenced by the absolute obligation of respect.

Thus, Conscience is "above the law." This is where Duty inverts itself into subjective self-will. The Conscience that is completely self-conscious becomes the "moral genius." This "Beautiful Soul" knows that it is hearing the voice of God in its Conscience. It still belongs to, and it speaks to and for, a community of conscientious respect; but it begins to resemble the Heart with its Law, because it is set apart from the rest of us who live by conventional standards.

The community for which the Beautiful Soul speaks becomes ever more *spiritual*—that is to say, not *here*, but imaginary. The presiding voice of the whole movement of Conscience is probably that of Jacobi, but the voice of Conscience as a Concept is that of Fichte; and the Beautiful Soul that hears only the sound of its own voice is that of Novalis (see the end of *Heinrich von Offterdingen*).

This beautiful soul is a "lost soul." It communes with its God and tells us what it hears. But it does not listen to what *we* say. So it has "trampled the roots of humanity underfoot" (W. and C. 51:23–24; Miller ¶69). Its God is really the pride of Lucifer. We have seen that the right of Conscience is fundamentally the right to justify having my own way. Hence, any Conscience can be assailed by the accusation of hypocrisy, and the Beautiful Soul ought to admit the justice of this accusation. But if it does that, it admits to being only the Heart with its own Law. That is to say, it admits to being *evil*. For no matter what it *does* to others, it is violating *their* hearts.

Now the final movement of *Forgiveness* begins. Whoever accuses the Beautiful Soul of hypocrisy is adopting the standpoint of judgement. That is not an active posture, but the posture of the observer. Thus, in showing the active Conscience that it is not "doing good," the judging consciousness ceases to do any good itself. Both of the two sides of the judgment are hypocrites. If we protest as agents that the judgment is an *act*, too, then we can see at once that it is the act of an evil will, for it chooses to focus on the selfish aspect of what Conscience justifies as well meant.

At this point, we must turn to the relation between the Beautiful Soul and the universal community of Conscience (from which it sundered itself and its ideal community of genius). From its judgment of the ordinary conscience, the Beautiful Soul becomes the Hard Heart and tramples the roots of humanity. The paradigm is Hölderlin's Hyperion, who tries to create the ideal community by direct political action. When defeated, he becomes the "hermit in Greece" and pronounces the verdict of damnation upon all of us moderns in the name of an ideal that is dead and gone.

The conscientious agent who confesses the inevitable imperfection of all her actions, because of their self-willed origin, expects to hear the judging consciousness express its own complementary imperfection. But this Hard Heart preserves itself in its literary fastness. It is here, in the pure linguistic world of the Spirit, that it must *break*. Through the ordinary experience of exchanging mutual forgiveness for our faults of perspective, we can pass on readily from the level of moral experience to that of Religion. But we cannot pass on to the Concept of Religion in its universal range unless we comprehend that world-historical Observation requires the complete surrender of moral judgement as a "valet's-eye view." The philosophical observer must fulfil the duty of forgiveness as completely as Jesus did on the Cross. Her standing assumption must be that only the universal spiritual aspect of what is observed matters. Every culture loves God as well as it can in its own way. Not only individual motives but also the moral biases of our own culture must be set aside.

What emerges directly at this point is the religious community of mutual forgiveness and universal charity. Forgiveness is the only moral duty that is truly *absolute*, for the willingness to enter even into the standpoint of the coward who saved his own life in the battle is the condition of truly human communication. This is the reality of moral respect. The coward must, of course, confess that he was a coward and that he needs forgiveness if the communication is to become perfect. But the spirit of the "reconciling Yes" that comes to birth in the handclasp of the agent and judge who do perfectly understand each other is the spirit of the God who died as a man on the Cross. Forgiveness is not only an absolute duty but also an absolute act of release. It cannot be conditional. Reciprocity is looked for, but it cannot be demanded.

Chapter 8
Religion

1. Absolute Selfhood

We saw at the beginning of chapter 7 that we were now observing "Shapes of a world," and we have now seen how the world of the self evolved from the simple identification of the *true* self with communal custom, through the alienated experience of legal and "divine" authority, to the identity of the self with its God in the Beautiful Soul. Finally, we have recognized God as the mediating "Spirit" who establishes the bond of linguistic communication between finite selves. This mediating spirit makes them brother and sister, because he is simply a human self like them who has passed over from natural selfhood to the spiritual community that the dead share with the living. Thus, the kind of communication that the absolute Spirit mediates is quite different from all of the ordinary finite communication of enlightened common sense. It is the restoration at the level of the universal rational community of the kind of *communion* enjoyed in an ideal family—the sort of perfect sympathy that is described in expressions such as "members one of another." This, of course, is also the ideal of the "Ethical Substance," but now the membership is in a universal community, not in finite communities that move against one another.

For the religious community, the mediating spirit is still an "other." He comes to them from beyond death—which marks his "absolute" otherness. Behind (or beyond) him there is the Other who *remains* in absolute otherness—the divine Lord whom we have met in several shapes already. Hegel's seventh chapter will be concerned with the mediation of all of those earlier shapes into the universal family of the human brother who achieved the absolute consciousness of forgiveness.

According to the enlightened analysis of Baron d'Holbach, "God" is the projected image of an idealized human self that is completely fictional. Hegel accepted the thesis of the projection, but not the view that the projection is a fiction. It is the finite human community that projects an image of its own infinite ground in thought—in other words, what is projected is not a dream image of what we wish for or what we fear, but the knowledge that we can achieve of what our world, and our life in it, is "in itself." This *includes* what we wish for and what we fear. But in their full, absolute context, these moments cease to be mere fictions, and in sofaras we discover them to be illusory in our experience with them, our conception of the absolute ground itself must change and develop. This is the "biography of God."

Since our experience of "God" is the evolution of the absolute Spirit that is the full self-consciousness of our own universally communal human Reason, the biography of God must follow the pattern of logical development that belongs to human Reason itself. But also, since what is evolving is now "the Whole"—or that which "truly is"—its evolutionary movement is very hard to observe and characterize logically. Within this absolutely universal "category of Being" all of the particular categories of experience are present, and they must evolve together. We always have to remember that it is our *present* culture with which we are concerned. It is the contribution that earlier cultures have made to the structure of our own lives that matters to us. Thus, the very fact that our observation is *phenomenological* implies that it is not logically *absolute*. There is no *absolute* truth of Egyptian, Greek, or medieval Catholic culture, and the speculative value of Hegel's logical characterization of the religions that are not essential contributors to our own cultural heritage is doubtful, or at least debatable. But, as we shall see, even the speculative interpretation of our own religious experience is essentially ambivalent, because the content of the universal speculative Concept that we establish as philosophical historians is the *personal* experience that we *must* be left to define conscientiously for ourselves.

In Hegel's logic of historical development, every cultural moment in the divine biography that ends at Calvary is determined by one of the *stages* of Consciousness, Self-Consciousness, and Reason. It is the Absolute Knowing of the philosophical community that is the religious consciousness of Spirit (and hence in the Logic we find the biography of God over again in correspondence with the evolutionary stages of Spirit).

2. Natural Religion

At its first appearance, the Absolute Spirit is simply the all-engulf-ing absolute Being (of Time) that we are primitively aware of in Sense-Certainty. The divine is a supersensible reality that reveals itself in the sensible world. This is the absolute consciousness of God as a "bad infinite beyond" which transcends our comprehen-sion. We *speak* of this power as a self, but since we do not yet have the awareness of ourselves as a "We that is I," our God cannot be a proper self. Hence, there is no "absolute Subject" in the natural religions who can *say* what "He" (and, implicitly, We) *is*. But for *us* (at the level of philosophical self-consciousness), Natural Religion *signifies* the philosophical proposition "Substance is the absolute essence" (see W. and C. 488:7–11 and 489:7–8; Miller ¶¶748–749). The perfect philosophical comprehension of this is Spinoza's *Natura naturans*. But the speculative proposition cannot be suc-cessfully asserted until that "first Substantiality" has been ne-gated; that is why Hegel says in the Preface, "the True is *not* Substance but just as much Subject." The use of "just as much" seems to imply "not *simply*," but that is not what is said (see W. and C. 14:2–3; Miller ¶17) and not quite what is meant. The for-mula in the Preface is a shorthand expression for: The True is not the original Substance, but the Subject that first radically negates that Substance and then develops into a new second Substance on its account. The emergence of the self-conscious Subject is the di-rect and immediate negation of Substance; their eventual equality grows up from the subjective extreme. (We shall see what this means in due course.)

The spiritual "sense-certainty" of the Absolute is the Universal Daylight emerging from Universal Night. Clearly, the Mosaic ac-count of the Creation is influential here; the Manifest Religion de-velops from historic Christianity, so its phenomenology must correspond logically with the Christian consciousness of its tradi-tion. Nevertheless, we should not identify the Daylight (or even the Night) with Yahweh (as W. Jaeschke has claimed), because Yahweh is *super*natural and cannot appear. (Hegel will refer to him in his proper place when we get to it.) The "Light Essence" is the Persian deity of Zoroaster.

This God is the absolute Lord; his manifest life is like fountains of fire, and his intellectual nature is simple sublimity (the Measureless). Since he is the immediacy of Spirit itself, we can think of him as the identity of Pleasure and Necessity. (The Pleasure is his, and the Necessity ours.)

This infinite fountain of Life must determine itself into particular shapes. Logically, it divides into the one universal Plant-Religion and the many particular Animal-Religions. The Plant-Religion belongs to the non-aggressive agriculturalists, and the Animal Religions belong to the warring tribes that identify themselves and their enemies as different species of living thing altogether. Yahweh, we may remember, is a war-god; the Israelites, on arriving in their land of milk and honey, had first to displace its peaceable inhabitants and then to fight with other imperialist invaders.

This is the religion of *Perception*. At the level of Self-Consciousness, we have the contrast between the harmony of Life and the Life-and-Death Struggle. Rationally, the Absolute observes itself (through us) as the River of Life and its mills; and spiritually, we are presented with the Heart's Law and the Frenzy of Self-Conceit. Empirically, this phase looks like imaginative armchair anthropology (which is not allowed), but it can be regarded as a guess at the early history of the Nile valley.

The religion of the Master Craftsman, to which we now pass, is certainly that of ancient Egypt, and it is the first one in which Hegel attempts to trace *development*. What is dominant here is the *instinctive* Understanding—that is, the Understanding as the instrument of our living needs. Society is a system of lordship and bondage; the plant-religionists become serfs bound to their land, and the warlike tribes become slave-craftsmen, each with the animal-gods of its craft. The "master craftsmen" themselves are the Priests who worship the Sun God (Daylight individualized) and mobilize the living community to build temples and tombs for the spiritual life in the darkness that lies beyond death. The Gods begin to assume a human form; but their eternal status is represented only by the homogeneous darkness of the "black stone" from which the statues are made. (It ought not to be necessary to say that there is *no* intended reference here to the unshaped Stone in Mecca.)

The revel of Life is here frozen into a caste system (the reference is to the second book of Herodotus and not to Hinduism, which cannot enter our story any more than Islam can). Apart from (Instinctive) Understanding, the moments realized here are Lordship and Bondage, Physiognomy and Phrenology (external relation of Soul and Body), and the immediate identity of Virtue with the Way of the World. The beginnings of Self-Conscious Art set up a properly continuous transition to the Art-Religion.

3. The Abstract Work of Art

At the point at which the Egyptian sculptor gives his God a human shape, a tremendous revolution is presaged. The Concept of the Divine Life in Nature is turned upside down. We go from Nature as *given* to Nature as *made*, and from the divine to the human concept of Law. The human community (actually Hellas) knows itself as *free*. This freedom is enjoyed by the Cities as independent communities, and it is consciously manifest to them in their Gods. Mortal individuals know themselves as organs of this communal freedom, which is represented for them by their artists (who must not represent themselves).

In its first manifestation, this aesthetic consciousness of freedom is represented "abstractly." That is to say, it is separated from finite life for contemplative awareness. *All* of Egyptian art is "abstract" in this sense, because it refers to the Beyond. But Greek "abstract art" refers to Greek life. The Greek deity (like the Egyptian) has a statue in her "house," but the house is her home *here*.

Inside the stone there is still only the darkness of death. But the people can give their God her voice by singing hymns communally for her (and in her praise). This is quite different from the oracular voice that already belonged to God in Nature and is carried over virtually unchanged, but the real oracle of God now is the voice that Antigone hears in her own mind.

There is an implicit contradiction between the Statue, which stably abides, and the Hymn, which dies away and is gone. The hymn is the first "true" being of God as Spirit, but this (anonymously communal) linguistic expression becomes stably individuated in the religious Cult. The universal Hellenic expression of this are the Mysteries of Eleusis, in which mortal individuals *purify* themselves (the symbolic expression of their "abstraction") and dedicate their lives to the Gods. It is impious to speak of the ceremonies, not because they are peculiarly secret, but because their meaning is to be expressed in active life. What actually *hap-*

pens occurs every day in the sacrifices (public and private), in which the useless parts of the animal given to the Gods are burned for their enjoyment but the rest is consumed by the worshippers. In this way, the God comes to be with her people.

The artist is recognized as the greatest giver of gifts to God. But the power to make the statue (or the hymn) comes from God, and anyone can offer anything to God (Heracleitus dedicated his book to Artemis at Ephesus). The transition from "abstraction" to actual life is made by virtue of the fact that everyone can help to build and decorate the temples—which, like the festivals, are completely public.

The Art-Religion is defined by its *Self-Consciousness*. In this first moment, we can recognize the perfection of *satisfied Desire* (the Mysteries being the Desire for another Self). In simple Consciousness, we are at the level of Perception (but the moments are hard to discriminate). By "abstraction" the art-work represents Rational Observation. Reason *finds* itself as the Spiritual Thing (inorganic, organic, self-actualizing); and, of course, the Olympian Gods portray the "Ethical Order" of True Spirit.

4. The Living Work of Art

In contrast to the *devotional* emphasis of the Abstract Work stands the direct expression of identity with God in the active life. This expression begins as an ecstatic identification with the powers of unconscious nature and moves through the self-conscious effort of the athlete to the great public processions in which every citizen lives out the experience of identity with the City's personified Substance. The processions for the drama festivals are included here, so the Art-Religion unfolds as an unbroken continuum.

This is where Yahweh makes his necessary conceptual appearance. According to Hegel's logic, there is an immediate identity between the pure *inner* and the pure *outer*, but they are experienced differently. Greek religion lacks the conscious awareness of *depth* (even if the depth is *empty* and hence only intellectually *sublime*). The Greek experience of depth is a *loss* of consciousness through a descent into the darkness of natural life. The Greeks and the Jews go in opposite directions from the universal Light of the Sunrise, and *enjoyment* is the right path.

In the darkness of unconsciousness it is Faust's Earth-Spirit that flourishes, with its masculine and feminine sides (Bacchus-Dionysus, and the Mother and Daughter of Eleusis). Wine brings the ecstatic union, and it is a circle of women that makes the "Bacchic revel" which was Hegel's famous image of the philosophic truth (W. and C. 35:16–19; Miller ¶47). Truth is born in the commitment to the dance of life.

But it is only the living spirit of family life that is manifested in this ecstasy. The great contests of the Olympic Games (and the other athletic festivals) brought all the Greeks together in a playful imitation of their masculine warlike existence; and the Olympic victor received almost the honours of a God. Whereas, within the City, the whole community (even the children) could go in procession with the God to celebrate her festivals. The Art-Religion was simultaneously both aristocratic-elitist and completely democratic.

But in none of this living activity is the perfect equality of mutual recognition adequately expressed. Language is the necessary medium for that. So the Spiritual Work of Art is *poetic*, and in particular it is a *play*. The Concept of Equal Recognition is the defining moment of this stage. Our spiritual Perception has achieved the perfect balance of Being-for-Other and Being-for-Self; Ethical Virtue maintains substantial Custom, and as the resolution of Ethical Action, we have the Syllogism of Marriage.

5. The Spiritual Work of Art

The climax of the Art-Religion is in the three moments of poetic expression: Universal-Epic, Particular-Tragic, and Singular-Comic. As "spiritual," the work of Art is distinct from actual life but not "abstract": It contains and expresses the whole experience of life. The tradition of the *Volk* begins with the great communal enterprise of the Trojan War, and in the Epic the action takes place on two levels (divine and human) in parallel. This is implicitly comic, because the Gods are supposedly immortal and belong to all of the contestants equally. The whole story is made by the Bard, but this human origin is not yet represented.

In Tragedy, it is the hero(ine) who speaks the poet's words; and the Chorus offers us the wisdom of the *Volk* against the Epic background. The careful economy of means (three actors) reduces the community of the Gods to a logical pattern. The Concept is split into its sides (as in the collision of the Laws in the *Antigone* or their reconciliation in the *Eumenides*). There are three essential moments: the two Laws and Zeus as the unity of the Substance. But the complementary opposition of human "knowledge" and "ignorance" (in the two sexes or in Family and Community) logically implies the downfall of the Substance, and the power of Fate is shown to be supreme over Zeus.

The actual shape of Fate is revealed in Comedy. Here, the actor peeps from behind the mask and lets us know that he is a mortal individual like ourselves. The Gods become the "Clouds," and the philosopher Socrates is the master of them all. The fate of the Art-Religion is to perish in pure thought. It offers us the perfect intuition of *Self-Conscious Freedom*: Epic love of Fate, Tragic making of Fate, and Comic self-recognition as Fate. Perception arrives at the Comedy of Common Sense, and Reason shows us the Cities as Spiritual Animals, the Lawgiving of Divine and Human Reason, and the Democratic Testing of the Laws. At the level of Spirit we have the motion of the downfall, seen from God's side: the Epic Recognition of the Dead Hero, the Tragedy of Ethical Action, and the Comedy of philosophical *status*.

6. The Emergence of the Manifest Religion

The Greek spirit could never have produced the "Man of Sorrows" in whom the Manifest Religion has its origin. He had to come from somewhere in the older world of the Sunrise. But Hegel regards him as a tragic hero translated from the stage into real life; this is what justifies his appearance in the running account of the Art-Religion (see W. and C. 460:33–461:17; Miller ¶703). The Manifest Religion (which we ought not to call "revealed") has a Hellenistic heritage (rather than the Jewish heritage that it purports to have).

Hegel did not divide his account of how Christianity evolved into the Manifest Religion of Reason. By this time, he was probably writing under severe deadline pressures; but we can conveniently distinguish in his discussion both the world-historical conditions for the appearance of this religion and the "belief of the World" in which it appeared from his systematic outline of its maturity.

The world of Comedy was a secular world. The "speculative proposition" of Comedy, "the Self is the absolute essence," is actually propounded by Socrates; it is philosophical rather than religious. This is the new beginning for the absolute Subject, after the effective negation of the Substance in the Art-Religion. This subjective proposition becomes properly religious in the Gospel, and in the religious shape, it contains its own inversion—the Unhappy Consciousness, in which the finite Self is reduced to a predicate of the absolute Substance. The Manifest Religion is the comprehensive inversion of both of these antithetic movements together, so that Absolute Spirit is the perfect equality of Subject and Substance.

We know already how the comedy of Stoicism and Scepticism becomes a tragic vision of religious despair. The Roman Emperor is the Comic self who gathers the Folk-Spirits into a Pantheon of abstract thought. The living Gods are all dead; this Hellenistic experience is the religious world-shape of the Unhappy Consciousness. The impulse that created great art has failed. The Virgin Mary (as Mother Church) now offers us the fruit plucked from the Greek poetic Tree of Knowledge, and we must recollect it rationally. The shapes of Hellenic culture and Imperial authority are all gathered around the cradle of Spirit—Bethlehem is a mythical image of Constantine's new City.

That the absolute substance of history has emptied itself out to become a human self can only come to consciousness after it has happened. But, in order for it to happen, the world must be ready for it. The Unhappy Consciousness that "God is dead" generates many dreams of his returning to save us. The spiritual world is full of Gnostic fancies that are visibly the work of the free imagination. It is out of this freely imaginative "nothing" that the absolute Spirit creates (or generates) itself in its own world. It has to follow the whole path of the phenomenology of finite consciousness in its evolution, because God must truly become finitely human in the process.

7. The "Belief of the World"

God's Incarnation happens through "the belief of the World." In other words, it begins with the Conversion of Constantine (who can speak for "the World") and the abandonment of the Imperial Cult. In dealing with the Unhappy Consciousness as a singular *Gestalt*, Hegel characterized this belief in the orthodox way. God came down and died as a man, far away and long ago. He has returned to his place, and only the grave remains here. But the "appearance" of the Manifest Religion is in the Faith for which the Saviour is still with us. Peter and the others who saw, heard, and touched the Saviour long ago still see and touch him; and we see, hear, and touch him too (in the Sacraments and the Book). He is *eternally* sensible. We cannot now *know* (in the historical sense) that the past tense ("they saw and touched him") is valid at all. But the essentially Gnostic "nothing" out of which the "belief" came is of no importance to us, because we know that he (and his disciples) are here *now*. God's Incarnation in *us* (as the mystic body of this present Saviour) is the simple content of the absolute Religion. Orthodox theology (as a theory *about* God) is part of the Perception and Understanding of this experience; Self-Consciousness arrives when we realize that, in "humbling himself" to the "form of a servant," God has actually "gone up" into his true essence. Reason dawns with the speculative theological concept of what has happened. Peter's recognition of Jesus as the Christ is the seed from which the speculative Concept was born, but Jesus did not become the Logos without undergoing a dialectical transformation. In the transforming process we can recognize the "second relation" of the Unhappy Consciousness as it was presented in Hegel's chapter IV. Hegel calls the "Shaped Unchangeable" "the *thing* of Perception" (W. and C. 497:34–36; Miller ¶762), so orthodox theology is actually the "sophistry" of our religious experience. The opposition of "this world" and "the Beyond" belongs to the movement of religious Understanding. Even Faith is not yet the proper conceptual Self-Consciousness of God as Spirit. We could see this in its struggle with Insight. Faith begins *from* the Unhappy Consciousness and is reduced to unhappiness again when its Beyond is taken from it; but it is then reborn as Rational Faith, and we have seen how that gives birth to the speculative Concept of God.

8. The Speculative Religion

In the speculative concept of Religion, the Trinitarian Faith that gave way to Insight becomes philosophical Logic. God as Speaker is emptied into the Word (i.e., Nature); and Nature exists concretely as our finite interpreting (which returns in its philosophical logic to the "Speech" of the Father). Thus, the absolute essence is properly the third Person (the Spirit). Hegel rejects the scientific atheism of someone like Kojève as the sundering of the "result" from its process. He has made clear from the beginning that this ought not to happen. God as Spirit is the God who is Love, because all of history must be preserved in its speculative significance. Logic *is* God's motion into Nature and history; but "He" is *us*, or the Spirit of our *absolute* community.

Set against the Heaven of Logic there must be the Earth of existence and singular representation. So God must be imagined as the "Creator"; this is a way of *representing* the logical necessity of self-othering and expressing the fact that the world can only exist *for* the Self. Similarly, the story of Eden and the Fall *represents* the logical necessities that Spirit must *emerge* from Nature and that the first condition of self-awareness must be the *knowledge* of our "nature" as evil. "Evil" is not simply "nothing." It is the active *negative* of the Good; and it belongs to God as his "wrath." But in our *knowledge* of it, it exists as already sublated.

In the process of the "estrangement" of Heaven and Earth, there must be two stages: the Unhappy Consciousness that only Heaven counts and the enlightened Happy Consciousness that only this world counts. But in the speculative reconciliation, the absolute and the finite spirit come together to their death upon the Cross.

What is born in the "Resurrection" from this death is Spirit in its mature shape as the universal community of the living and the dead. It is for this universal community of forgiveness that the *Vorstellung* of the birth, death, and Resurrection exists in its proper interpretation. This community can *say* that God always was the Logos and the Logos always was human, but it cannot *comprehend* what it says. The speculative truth is there, but it has not yet been consistently interpreted—in particular, the existence of evil and its relation to God have not been comprehended properly.

Implicitly, however, the resolution is at hand, because the present Saviour is the recognized Self of his community. The finite self must return to him and know itself in him; and in this process every element in the *Vorstellung* (from Adam and Eve to the Crucifixion) receives an opposite value *in addition* to the one that it obviously has. Every moment becomes dialectical (as it has done for us already). Thus, what appears as our "Fall" is the freedom through which we can die to sin without dying naturally. This is a different withdrawal into self from that of the Hard Heart (not to speak of the natural self). Resurrection is a communal experience in the here and now; God's death and resurrection as a man becomes the universal experience of every day. There are not two species of humanity—the embodied and the "risen"—but a dying and resurrection for me now. Jesus, as a man, was the one-sided insistence that only the Kingdom of God matters. Both he and the Father with whom he was "one" are now dead together, but the darkness of this night is the breath of the true Resurrection at Pentecost.

Now Hegel can make his transition to Absolute Knowing. He has shown that absolute Spirit is the self-knowing process that unites the three moments. It is the mover, the movement, and the medium (or substance) in which the moving happens. We have come back to the "Yes" of situated Freedom from which this chapter began. But for the community, the content still exists as images of a divine and human history. It has transcended the natural meaning of the images, but it still uses them. So the community is not *presently* self-conscious. It is still in a state of Faith. It is conscious of the movement as originating "from above" and as directed towards the future. The immediate sense of God's presence has still to spell itself out in a reconciliation of the world with itself.

In the three moments of the movement we can recognize the full shape of *Reason*. The first moment gives us Observing Reason accompanied by the first phases of Understanding (Force as mutual solicitation) and Unhappy Consciousness (God as Fate's Judgement). The second moment is dominated by the story of the God-Man: The Crucifixion is the surrender of Pleasure to Necessity, the Resurrection is the triumph of the Heart over Self-Conceit, and Pentecost is the return of Virtue to the World. The third moment is the Community of Reason: The religious community is the *Sache selbst*, Reason's Law is the law of universal Charity, and the "Test of Reason" is the forgiving of trespasses. The rest of the pattern cannot be clearly discerned. Hegel did not articulate this part of the chapter sufficiently for us to recognize the three stages of its *spiritual* structure.

Chapter 9
Absolute Knowing

1. The Recapitulation

In the last section of Hegel's seventh Chapter we noticed that the articulation of the argument was failing. Hegel wrote the last part of his manuscript in a hurry, because of his promise to supply the completed book by a definite date in October of 1806. He would certainly have written at greater length in his last chapter had it not been for this promise, but we must make out the argument as well as we can. The only problem that now remains is the closure of the Science of Experience into a proper circle. The Self of Cognition has been shown to be the mediating moment between the finite spirit and the absolute Spirit. It is the self of the infinite community—the incarnate Logos, the "I that is We." Now we have to show (on the one hand) how this absolute Concept comprehends all the experiences that have led us to it and (on the other hand) how we, as singular consciousness, actually comprehend it. We all embody the Concept (before we do any philosophizing at all) because it comprehends us—that is, it provides the context of all that we intelligently say and do, and of everything that we understand about what is unintelligent. But to embody it *as a Concept* is to raise it to the level of explicit self-consciousness on its theoretical side.

The spirit of the Manifest Religion has not recognized its conscious object as its own *self*. The community of Absolute Spirit is an image for this, and because of our return to the real community of forgiveness, we know that the form of the final transformation must have appeared already. The object of devotion is an object of spiritual sense, but it is also perceptual, because it is in itself what it is for another; and as a whole it is a syllogistic process that goes from the Universal to the Singular and back. We must pick out the moments in our earlier progression that will articulate these aspects for us, and we need only be concerned with our finite side of the problem here—that is, with phenomenology, not with logic.

The object of sense is the human saviour as dead. We came to that moment universally at the climax of Phrenology. The human self is Yorick; our singularity is identical with our "thinghood." But, as is always true of thinghood, this sensible being has meaning only through the relation of the Ego to it as active; the Concept of Utility is the rational shape of perceptible being. Finally, the sensible thing has to be understood as the essence of the self. This happened for us in the stabilization of the moral self as Conscience (the finite embodiment that must be respected). The reconciliation of the ideal world of religious devotion with its actual world is built from these three elements. We begin from Conscience because it contains the first two sublated. It is the perfection of Conscience in Forgiveness that gives rise to the singular self as the pure knowing of the community. Religion brought us back to this. So the identity of the two movements must now be demonstrated. In Religion, the movement appears as voluntary on the side of God, but its proper form is that which it has on our side—that is, the voluntary motion of the Beautiful Soul. The self-absolution of forgiveness is a death of self that must now go on to become pure knowing. Reconciliation in finite action becomes reconciliation with the universal order of being in order to know it.

2. Science as Self-Comprehension

Hegel clearly says that this equalization of the finite subjective standpoint with the religious objective one is a "shape of spirit" (W. and C. 523:1; Miller ¶797). But given its two-sided origin, it is not surprising that we must say that under one aspect it is a "shape" and under another it is not. The philosopher is a singular shape of consciousness, and in her perfect appreciation of the great circle of experience, she is logically the richest of all shapes; but when she moves on to develop the Science of Logic from the threshold provided by the standpoint of speculative observation that we have now achieved, she is "pure thinking"—and that is a "shape" no longer, because "experience" is left behind.

The fact that we have now reached the position of self-conscious comprehension of our own standpoint as speculative "observers" of experience is the key to the puzzle about how "the Absolute is with us from the start" (W. and C. 58:10–11; Miller ¶73). One cannot do "science" without knowing how to be a neutral observer; of course, one makes mistakes and suffers from biases, but one is prepared to have them pointed out and to recognize the justice of the correction, or at least (in the event of a continuing disagreement), to admit the validity of the opposing point of view when one's own arguments fail to convince the opponent. In the last resort, one is prepared to forgive what appears as obstinate persistence in an illogical position—but at that point we leave the level of Absolute Knowing and return to that of Religion.

Our only remaining "object" at this level is the logical movement of self-sublation, which "we" have been throughout the process of Spirit's appearing. This is the shape of the Concept in its objectivity. We can easily appreciate that this Concept could not have appeared any sooner than it did, because the experience of the religious community had to be mature and the speculative interpretation of it had to be developed. The Gospel had to be proclaimed and Platonically interpreted in an imaginative mode; the subjective consciousness had to advance gradually from imagination to conceptual thinking. Through this historical development, human self-consciousness finally arrives at comprehension of the "whole" within which it begins as consciousness. (This is Hegel's own material explanation of how "the Absolute is with us from the start" [W. and C. 524:33–35; Miller ¶801].)

Development in time is the necessary actual form of the Spirit, and that is why all knowledge comes from "experience." But in Hegel's *"spiritual* empiricism," this applies just as much to the *form* of truth as it does to the content. Form and content develop together. That is the *philosophical* truth of experience. Hegel gives us a bird's-eye view of the gradual emergence of the speculative standpoint since Descartes to support and illustrate this claim. Clearly, he takes the work of Descartes to be the moment when the Christian experience became decisively philosophical and the speculative identity of consciousness with God was born. Perhaps this is only the subjective (i.e., inadequately historical) truth of his own personal development, or perhaps he could have given us a more complete account had he not been forced to abbreviate his discussion so radically. But at least his determination to validate the experience of Natural Religion philosophically is evident. Now that we have grasped the logical wholeness of our experience, we must go down into the depths of social memory fearlessly; we shall not be drowned in the "dark night where all the cows are black" (W. and C. 13:21–24 and 527:11–26; Miller ¶¶16 and 803), because we are now the subjectivity of the Substance. W have comprehended the whole.

3. The Circle of Experience

The *Phenomenology* ends by demonstrating the closure of the circle of experience. Hegel wants to show us briefly how the circle comprehends the whole range of philosophy as a logical system. In this connection, he makes a puzzling comment about the existence of a parallel between the shapes of experience and the conceptual moments of the Science of Logic. We cannot now discover how he envisaged this, because he never referred to it again in any version of his later Logic. Probably he abandoned the idea; the only vestige of it is the parallel between the movement of the Logic and that of the history of philosophy which we find in his Berlin lectures. He also indicates a parallel between the motion of the Logic and that of the biography of God in the *Encyclopaedia*. But he does not exhibit it properly, and it is not strictly chronological, in the way that the movement of chapter VII of the *Phenomenology* is.

In the *Logic*, the dialectical motion is strictly conceptual; there is no interaction with historical experience. But from the claim for a perfect parallel we can infer that at least the beginning and the terminus must be the same, and this inference is confirmed by the climactic return to Absolute Knowing in the Science of Logic. Speculative Logic moves from Absolute Knowing as the standpoint of the philosophical historian in the *Phenomenology* to its own conceptual appreciation of the method of philosophical thinking as absolute cognition.

As far as the Philosophy of Nature is concerned, we have already seen (in the exposition of the Manifest Religion) that the externalization of pure thinking into the otherness of Nature is logically necessary. In my opinion, this is interesting only as a theological proposition about God; from the experiential standpoint of finite spirit, it is obvious that we cannot come to the speculative consciousness of the absolute selfhood of the human scientific community unless we begin with the awareness of ourselves as finite consciousnesses in the natural order. What is important for us is that our natural sense-experience is already the experience of freedom. The scientific consciousness (or natural religious consciousness) of ourselves as puppets in the grip of natural necessity (or fate) is already an *alienated* mode of awareness. This is the fundamental reason why the Hellenes were, for Hegel, the paradigm of "natural consciousness."

The formation of what we can conveniently call the Spinozist concept of God as Nature is the absolute encounter of knowledge with its own limit; at this point a reversal must begin. This is where the *philosophical* breach between Nature and Spirit is made; the movement of scientific subjectivity begins here. We can now appreciate properly the moving record of human freedom in history. The philosophy of Spirit recapitulates the journey of philosophical experience from simple sense-consciousness all the way to the great "procession of Spirits" in the last paragraph. The Lectures on Art, Religion, and Philosophy will expand the apparent range of the procession. But if I am right in thinking that all the *Gestalten* of Consciousness are included here, then it is the phenomenological procession that is truly comprehensive.

We have never ceased to be the sense-certain self that embarked on the journey. Now, therefore, as we recollect the course of human religious and cultural history, we are appreciating the world (natural and spiritual) in its full extent, and it now belongs self-consciously to us as our *human* "substance." The *Phenomenology* is Hegel's "philosophy of history" in the properly speculative sense in which "history" comprehends all the modes of human cognitive experience. What is called the "philosophy of world-history" inside the System is only one aspect of this comprehensive Concept. It has the determinate function of moving us from the sphere of Objective Spirit to that of Absolute Spirit, and in doing that it shows how "freedom" is an objectively real concept in experience, not merely a regulative ideal. It is the *Phenomenology* that is a true organon of historical knowledge.

For this reason, the *Phenomenology* provides the right key for the estimation of the "eternal" significance of the System itself. As the speculative comprehension of time in eternity and eternity in time, the *Phenomenology* is "eternal" in a way in which the systematic comprehension of Hegel's own time in the System cannot be. We shall see in our concluding chapter that in the perspective of the Science of Experience many of the familiar complaints about Hegel's overweening intellectual pride are quite mistaken. But the main implication of that insight will be that the "Real Philosophy" of the System is no longer directly relevant to the problems of our time. In the "real philosophical" sense, we have to achieve the comprehension of our own time for ourselves. The "comprehension of time" in the *Phenomenology* is *absolute*; it cannot suffer historical sublation in that same way. This is the "absolute knowledge" that it has brought us.

Chapter 10
The *Phenomenology* and the System

1. The *Phenomenology* and the "Real Philosophy"

The *Phenomenology* was conceived as both the introduction for and the "first part" of a "system of philosophy." Its introductory function is easy to comprehend, because it leads us from our normal "enlightened common sense" to the standpoint of Absolute Knowing from which the "pure thinking" of speculative Logic begins. It is the "ladder" for this, which rational common sense is entitled to demand (see W. and C. 20:6–8; Miller ¶26). Its status as "first part" can best be grasped by recognizing that it is the "theory of appearance," while the System is the "theory of reality." It is *coordinate* with the System as a whole; both of them have the same universal scope, but their approaches are from opposite directions. Phenomenology moves away from actual experience towards pure logic; the System moves from pure Logic back to real experience.

Hegel's plan exhibited this coordinate conception at the time that the book was published. The "system of speculative philosophy" was to be completed in one more volume containing both the speculative Logic and the "Real Philosophy" of Nature and Spirit. But the writing of the *Logic* cost him much hard labour, and (like the *Phenomenology* before it) the work grew far beyond its expected bulk. It was eventually published in three volumes between 1812 and 1816.

At that point, Hegel was finally called to a regular post as a philosophy professor. He needed a *systematic* handbook for his lectures, so he rapidly produced the first version of the *Encyclopaedia*. By that time he had realized that the *Phenomenology* was not a very convenient "introduction to speculative philosophy" for pedagogical use, so it is not surprising that he supplied something much simpler for the expanded second edition of the *Encyclopaedia* in 1827. But even there he made clear that in his eyes the *Phenomenology* was still a valid *scientific* approach to speculation (*Enz.*

§25); and in the last year of his life he began to prepare new editions of both of his first big books.

His work on the *Phenomenology* did not go far, but we can see that he intended to delete all references to its being either "part" of the System or the "introduction" to it. With his new, much simpler, and more contemporary introduction to the *Encyclopaedia*, he had made the System completely self-sufficient and independent. From notes that he made for the presentation of the new edition of the *Phenomenology*, we can see that he was also troubled about the "revolutionary Napoleonic" tenor of the "science of experience." In the changed world of the Restoration, he needed to apologize for this. But the only rational conclusion that can be drawn from his decision to republish the book in spite of that difficulty is that he still regarded the "science of experience" as a valid project in itself, and as one which he had completed in a fairly adequate way.

The fact that "Phenomenology" forms one phase of the systematic philosophy of Subjective Spirit (*Enz.* §§413–439) is completely irrelevant to the problem of the status of the 1807 *Phenomenology* in relation to the *Encyclopaedia* of 1827 and 1831. It is obvious that the development of the "finite spirit" is a necessary topic in the systematic theory of the relation between Nature and Spirit; we find it dealt with in this context in the "systems" that Hegel drafted both before he wrote the "Science of the Experience of Consciousness" and while he was writing it. There would, in all probability, have been a "Phenomenology" of the finite subjective Spirit in the systematic volume that was projected to accompany the *Phenomenology of Spirit*. The book title—decided upon only after the Science was complete—refers to the Universal Spirit (i.e., the World-Spirit), not to the finite Spirit. The development of Spirit does, of course, partially coincide in the two perspectives, but the purpose that defines the undertaking as a whole is quite different.

Now that we have gotten that red herring out of the way, let us consider the relation between the *Phenomenology* and the "real philosophy" of Objective Spirit. The *Philosophy of Right* provides the fullest account of Hegel's mature theory here, and it is in his "Introduction" to that work that Hegel says, "Philosophy is its own time comprehended in thoughts." This remark defines the whole project of "Real Philosophy" perfectly; and it shows us the difference between that work and the *Phenomenology* and *Logic*.

Far from being "the comprehension of its own time," the *Logic* is "the thought of God before the Creation." It is *our* thought, but it is the comprehension of "eternity." The *phenomenological* "Science of Experience" is neither the comprehension of its own time nor the comprehension of eternity, but the universal comprehension of time as such. It has to be the comprehension of its own time—incidentally but essentially—because it must begin from there, and all of the "recollecting" that it involves must necessarily be done in the perspective of that particular time. We may well see Athens and Jerusalem (for example) in quite a different light from that in which Hegel sees them, and the general perspective on the French Revolution had changed dramatically already by the time Hegel died. So we have to study the time in which the book was written with real historical devotion in order to comprehend it properly. But the lessons that we can learn from it are not time bound in the way that those of the "Real Philosophy" necessarily are.

In this perspective, it is crucial that everything in the *Phenomenology* prior to the world of Conscience and the Beautiful Soul is dead and gone; it must be *resurrected* (As Hegel saw it) in our own imaginative recollection. The objective world of the Real Philosophy, however, was all present to Hegel; and now that it is gone, our own perspective upon it has become phenomenological. A perfect paradigm of what this means is provided by Antigone. Hegel regarded the incursion of Antigone into the political arena as both logically and naturally inevitable; but Sophocles did not see it in that light. For him it constituted her tragic error, and it is only by accepting his view of her "proud thoughts" (*Antigone*, line 1350) that we can properly give her a place beside Helen and Jocasta in "the eternal irony of the community" (W. and C. 314:1–21; Miller ¶475). What Antigone wanted (what she was pleading for in the sophistical speech that Hegel misunderstood) was a community in which she would not be *forced* to act politically, because the pieties of her family life would be respected. Thus, Hegel does better justice to Antigone's incipient "morality" when he makes her the ideal model of true womanhood in his Real Philosophy. But for us, it is the perspective of the *Phenomenology* that is *eternally* valid. Our heroine is the political "sinner" against *Sittlichkeit* both in its natural and its "returned" Hegelian shape, and the logic of the *Phenomenology* shows that this is not just a truth for *our* time (as against Hegel's).

Again, the complete transformation of international war in our century has shown us that we can no longer regard war as the "infinite" moment in a providentially rational system for the maintenance of social health in the finite community. The world of Hegel's Philosophy of Spirit perished between 1914 and 1945.

Since 1918, even the central concept of the political State has suffered a radical inversion, for which speculative comprehension is still lacking. Hegel's National State is supposed to sublate the Civil Society in which the national economy is articulated; but the economy was always implicitly universal (international), and now it is explicitly so. It is now the case, therefore, that Civil Society sublates the State, rather than vice versa. We can still go to the *Phenomenology* for an evolutionary theory of the moments that have to be restored to harmony in any new equilibrium, and since the *Phenomenology* did not need the theory of the rational State for its own completion, we must integrate the *Philosophy of Right* into it for this purpose. But the relation between the two works (as far as the relevance of Hegel for our time is concerned) is quite the opposite of what the idolaters of the *Encylopaedia* typically assume to be the case.

When we come down to the details, it must also be recognized, that much of the "application" of Hegel's speculative theory, seeking to show that "the actual is rational," was nothing more than "rationalization" even in his own time. The nobility, as it existed in the world of the Restoration, was a survival from the world of the Ancien Régime. When we look at it in the light of the *Phenomenology*, we have to agree with the criticism that was already levelled at the *Philosophy of Right* by the young Karl Marx. Further, it seems to me that Spaventa was right in claiming that the death penalty is inconsistent with Hegel's essentially *educational* philosophy of punishment. This is not difficult to see when that theory is set into the context of the great arc that goes from the Life-and-Death Struggle to Universal Forgiveness. The death penalty implicitly involves a kind of social bondage-relation which is at odds with the principle of conscientious recognition; and that principle is the ultimate criterion of political rationality.

When we move downwards from Spirit to Nature, the story is the same. Obviously, the great revolutions in chemistry, biology, and physics have caused Hegel's *actual* philosophy of Nature to be

completely superannuated; but we have seen that the general doctrine of the identity of life with its environment in the *Phenomenology* can readily be adjusted to accommodate the Darwinian
revolution. The threat to our living environment posed by the
great increase in human technological power has necessitated a
radical inversion of the traditional view of Nature as the stable
backdrop of our lives. For the future, we must conceive of our
place in Nature in practical (i.e., morally responsible) terms, but it
is still the "identity theory" of objective idealism that we require
for the practical Philosophy of Nature that we must now construct.
That "Concept" is articulated better in Hegel's *Phenomenology* and
Logic than it is anywhere else. The more Hegel's "Real Philosophy" takes on the aspect of a historical curiosity, the more evident
does the relevance of his logical theory to our situation become.
Even his "elements"—Earth, Air, Water, and Fire—are as significant for "environmental studies" as they are absurd in our Chemistry.

2. The *Phenomenology* and the *Logic*

We have now seen why Hegel's *Phenomenology* is more directly
relevant to the problems of our own later age than his "Real Philosophy" can ever be. But what is the status of his "Logic of Reality" in relation to his "Logic of Appearance"? It has been one
principal object of this short book to show that the "absolute knowing" of appearances provides the ideal standpoint both for the
appreciation of our own experience and for the objective situating
of our practical relations with the community and with our fellows as individuals. What more do we need? *Our* science is supposed to be the "introduction" to the speculative logic that we
should use in the systematic interpretation of our real world. But
is that purely conceptual logic really possible? Is it not really a
"bad infinite" task? Must we not do "Real Philosophy" over and
over again as the times change, using always the best concepts that
experience has given us? Is the Science of Experience itself the only
completable science?

    Obviously, Hegel did not think so. But no one (as far as I know)
has yet explicated the relation of the *Logic* to the Real Philosophy
in a convincing way, and even if this could be done for the System
that Hegel actually produced, I do not see how the "eternal" valid-

ity of the *Logic* would be established thereby. The situation might well be that the Hegelian *Logic* would be dragged down into the timebound status of the Real Philosophy that it articulates. If we are to defend the unity and integrity of Hegel's speculative Logic as a proper science, we must turn back and examine its relation to the other logical science, the one that has successfully completed itself.

The "absolute knowing" of the *Phenomenology* is articulated by the philosopher for the community of those whose aim it is to observe the world (or some aspect of it) *sub specie aeternitatis*. When the speculative philosopher moves on from being an "observer" to the pure thinking of Logic, we must assume that it is the structure of her scientific community's life in the world that she is articulating. For that is what has been shown to be "what truly is." This is what explains the effort that Hegel made for more than twenty years to simplify his Logic, and to concentrate it as much as possible, so that it could be learned by students. Everyone who enters the University is vocationally destined for membership in the community of "absolute knowing." The Logic was presented to the learner in Hegel's time as a theory of the divine nature—a serial development of the concept of God, in which every movement to a new level gives us a new "definition." But as the concept of God advances, the learner's relation to it changes; and when the climax is reached with the concept of pure thinking itself as a *method*, the last vestige of the traditional concept of God has vanished.

When we present the Logic to the student now, we do not need the theological underpinning at all. We have only to make sure that she understands that she is studying the structure of the community of which she is already a rational member, with the object of becoming more completely self-conscious in her membership. The living Earth is the being that is the "body" of this community on its natural side, and the student can use any symbols that her own cultural tradition has given her to express the unity of the body on its spiritual side.

That the community *has* an ideally permanent logical structure, in its passage from the natural "body" to the spiritual one, is guaranteed by her own embodiment as a student. The rational structure of selfhood, the paradoxical union of singularity and universality in community membership, the identity of "the We that is I and the I that is We" is the key to what is "logically necessary." This is the heart and centre of philosophical logic, and it is safe from the continual change and transformation that must be dominant in Real Philosophy, because the structure of our embodied life-experience will not change. No matter what may happen to our rational world at the level of scientific Understanding, we must continue to live in the world of Sense-Certainty and Perception, the world of common sense and real life, in which we struggle to assert ourselves, are disciplined by our elders, and finally collaborate in a system of (debatably and contentiously) "equal recognition." In this stable world, we must contribute to, and reliably maintain, the structures of Objective Spirit which the good life (shockingly *bad*, perhaps, in our own eyes) has been shown to require. Wherever our scientific conceptualization of "nature" (either the universal order or our own particular nature) may lead our thoughts, the necessary second inversion of the Scientific Understanding will always restore the primacy of the standpoint of ordinary human life. For practical (technological) reasons, the natural-scientific viewpoint has to remain somehow continuous with the conceptual system that we use in our everyday lives (both physical and spiritual). Therefore, the logical categories that *human* life and *human* communication require must remain fundamental (even though there are already important forms of communication that do not use them).

The reliable permanence of philosophical logic depends upon the necessary primacy of "real life" and its *ordinary* language; and that primacy means that—in defiance of common sense itself—the universal concept of Nature is really *human*. This is the ultimate significance of the "Inverted World," and it is the reason why speculative logic is a completable Science. It turns out that the *Phenomenology* provides the most reliable criterion of what belongs properly to the *Logic* and what belongs to the Real Philosophy. Only by regarding the Science of Logic and the Science of Experience as a conceptual circle can we defend the integrity of the Hegelian logic.

To expound the dialectic of "pure thinking" at its three levels of Being, Essence, and Concept would require another book, but we may notice two important points here. First, since the perceptual *thing* already *has* an "essence" (and the Concept of Force *is* an "essence"), any *parallel* between the *Phenomenology* and the *Logic* in 1806 must have been rather peculiar—and probably not sequen-

tial, since we encounter the "laws of thought," which are fundamental to the logic of "essence," only in the Self-Observation of
Reason. Secondly, the Pure Being with which Logic begins must
(as Spaventa argued) be the being of pure thinking contemplated
as an object by the thinker. For this is where the *Phenomenology*
terminates. The Science of Logic makes a perfect circle, returning
to the pure thinking of the dialectical method; and the opening
discussion of the question "With what must the Science begin?" is
only a piece of Aristotelian dialectic designed to help those who
have not studied the full "introduction to Logic."

3. The Philosophy of Absolute Spirit

Felix Mendelssohn wrote to his sisters from Naples in May of 1831
that, with Goethe still alive and Beethoven only recently dead, it
was madly funny to hear that Hegel was declaring German art to
be "dead as mutton" (in German, *mausetot*; see G. Nicolin, report
669). We do not know what Hegel was actually saying, because
accurate transcripts of his lectures have not yet been published.
But when we read, in the edition that we do have, "Art is for us a
thing of the past" (*T.W.-A.* 13, p. 25; Knox, p. 11), we can see that he
is speaking, first, about the ideal of beauty that we received from
the Greeks, and, second, about the supersession of the "Beautiful
Soul" in the "absolute knowing" of the philosopher. Nowhere (in
what is published) does he mean what Mendelssohn took him to
mean. In the same context from which I have quoted, he says, "We
may well hope that art will always rise higher, and come to perfection." So if he ever did say what Mendelssohn ascribes to him, he
has already agreed that he was crazy. For he certainly agreed that
Goethe was the greatest poet that Germany had produced.

We can use the *Phenomenology* to defend the thesis that Art dies
twice in Hegel's ideal biography of the World-Spirit. First it dies
with the Art-Religion. In the Greek world the artist was the "maker
of Gods." It was through Art that the Gods (and their worshippers) became truly *humane*. One cannot say that Art *created* the
Gods, for the "natural religions" existed before Homer or any
other recognizably self-conscious poet. But Art created the di-
vinely human (or humanly divine) *consciousness* of the Gods, and
that function is over and done.

But that first "death" occurred at the moment when Art itself was born as an *independently* free mode of Absolute Spirit. We cannot worship Zeus, as Antigone did, but we can recognize Sophocles as a supreme artist; and we cannot approve of the Athenian prosecution of Pheidias for the crime of placing his own image on Athena's shield, because we must condemn the *fatwa* against Salman Rushdie as an ugly and reactionary blot upon human Reason. The religious conception of Art is immature.

The Art that was *liberated* in Greek Comedy went into the voluntary *service* of the Christian Saviour, but in the Renaissance, the spirit of Christian Art ("Romantic Art," as Hegel called it) was properly liberated again. Its second "death" (in the Beautiful Soul and in the spirit of *irony*) is strictly conceptual. It goes hand in hand with the "death of God" in Faith, which marks the transition from Faith to speculative insight as the "element" of Religion; and just as the "death of God" is not final, neither is the death of Romantic Art. God and Man are resurrected together in the rational ideal of the Community; and Art must logically be resurrected with the task of portraying that community in the infinite variety of its aspects. That is what our hope for Art's future rise towards perfection means.

When we move on with the Absolute Concept from Art to Religion, we encounter a different problem. Here we must find Hegel guilty of an illegitimate extension of the phenomenological method. The *Lectures on the Philosophy of Religion* are structured *phenomenologically*. We can see this most clearly in the placement of the Roman "religion of expediency." But when Hegel extends the range of his observation (as the *systematic* treatment of Religion requires) to embrace the living world-religions other than Christianity, this phenomenological perspective leads to the projection of cultural imperialism (prevalent in European culture from the time of the Crusades onwards) upon the non-Christian world. The great religions of the East are interpreted simplistically in terms of the elementary categories of Being, and a new Gnostic myth of the supposed "march of the Spirit" from East to West is invoked in order to justify this radical departure from the fundamental Hegelian insight that "the essence should be grasped as the unity of thinking and time" (W. and C. 527:2–4; Miller ¶803).

Since cultures must be arrayed somehow in the System, and the Eastern societies are still "substantial" with respect to recognition—or at least that is how they appear to us—Hegel's logical typology of religions could perhaps be provisionally allowed as *valid for us*. But the *Phenomenology* itself logically imposes the task of unpacking the structure of each religious community into a full display of its moments; and, of course, this can only be done from inside by a philosophical participant in the culture. Hegel understood that well enough; but it is only in our time that the urgent need for a systematic comprehension of cultural differences based on the principle of conscientious (i.e., spiritually equal) recognition has become apparent. Hegel's way of ordering cultures on a scale of development is not helpful for us; indeed, it is an obstacle to mutual understanding. But his view of what religious experience is shows the way towards a humane continuum of effective communication. His own conception of philosophical "system" in this area was determined by the fact that his time was precisely the one in which the "phenomenology of Spirit" was discovered. But the perfect development of the concept of Recognition in his book is the proper key for the overturning of his systematic "realization" of Absolute Spirit in favour of one that is more truly Absolute.

Hegel was a man of his time, not least in his enlightened optimism. He was confident that no second "revolution" would be needed after that of 1789 and that no civilized nation which had felt the full impact of that upheaval could possibly fall back into the political despotism which he thought of as barbaric. The experience of this century has shown how badly mistaken he was, but his mistake was essentially *empirical*. There is nothing in his logical theory to warrant the belief that the motion of consciousness must always be progressive. Every position of consciousness contains the earlier positions in a sublated form, and every position is a stable circle that can maintain itself against criticism. Thus stability is "natural," and regression is just as possible as progress. When Fackenheim claims that if Hegel were alive today he would not be a Hegelian, he is right in thinking that Hegel would not believe (as perhaps in his own time he did) in the "march" of a transcendent Spirit around the world with the Sun—and logically *forwards* in history. But that was only Hegel's "religion" (if indeed he had one that went beyond what was philosophically demonstrable). Hegel the *philosopher* could still maintain his position without change. It has been the object of this little book to make clear what that *philosophical* position is.

A Short Bibliography

Except for the basic texts, this list is restricted almost entirely to works that will be found useful by students who are not yet well versed in the study of Hegel.

1. The Basic Texts

G. W. F. Hegel: *Gesammelte Werke*, ed. Rheinisch-Westfaelischen Akademie der Wissenschaften, Hamburg, F. Meiner, 1968ff. This is the critical edition, which is still in the process of publication. *Phänomenologie des Geistes* appears in volume 9.

G. W. F. Hegel: *Werke in zwanzig Bänden*, ed. E. Moldenhauer and K.M. Michel, Frankfurt-am-Main, Suhrkamp Verlag, 1970–1971 (Theorie Werkausgabe). This is the most readily available edition for everything not yet published in the *Gesammelte Werke*. The *Phänomenologie des Geistes* is Band 3; and the *Enzyklopädie* (abbreviated *Enz.*) is Bände 8–10.

G. W. F. Hegel: *Vorlesungen*, 10 vols., various eds., Hamburg, Meiner, 1983ff.

G. W. F. Hegel: *Phänomenologie des Geistes*, ed. H.-F. Wessels and H. Clairmont, Hamburg, F. Meiner, 1988. This is the student edition based upon volume 9 of *Gesammelte Werke*. All references to the German text in the present book are to this edition (abbreviated as "W. and C.").

G. W. F. Hegel: *Briefe von und an Hegel*, 4 vols., ed. Johannes Hoffmeister and Rolf Flechsig, Hamburg, F. Meiner, 1961.

G. Nicolin, ed.: *Hegel in Berichten seiner Zeitgenossen*, Hamburg, F. Meiner, 1970.

2. Translations

G. W. F. Hegel: *The Letters*, trans. Clark Butler and Christiane Seiler, commentary by Clark Butler, Bloomington, Indiana University Press, 1984.

G. W. F. Hegel: *Phenomenology of Spirit*, trans. A. V. Miller, with introduction and analysis by J. N. Findlay, Oxford, Clarendon Press, 1977.
References to the paragraph numbers of this translation are given throughout the present book.

G. W. F. Hegel: *Early Theological Writings*, trans. T. M. Knox, with an introduction and fragments translated by Richard Kroner, Chicago, University of Chicago Press, 1948; reprinted Philadelphia, University of Pennsylvania Press, 1971.

G. W. F. Hegel: *Three Essays* 1793–1795 (Tübingen fragments, Life of Jesus), trans. Peter Fuss and John Dobbins, Notre Dame, Indiana, Notre Dame University Press, 1984.

G. W. F. Hegel: *Difference Between the Systems of Fichte and Schelling*, trans. H. S. Harris and Walter Cerf, Albany, State University of New York Press, 1977.

G. W. F. Hegel: *Faith and Knowledge*, ed. and trans. W. Cerf and H. S. Harris, Albany, State University of New York Press, 1977.

G. W. F. Hegel: "Relation of Scepticism to Philosophy" (trans. H. S. Harris), in G. di Giovanni and H. S. Harris, trans. and ann., *Between Kant and Hegel, Texts in the Development of Post-Kantian Idealism*, Albany, State University of New York Press, 1985.

G. W. F. Hegel: *Political Writings*, trans. T. M. Knox, with an introductory essay by Z. A. Pelczynski, Oxford, England, Clarendon Press, 1964.

G. W. F. Hegel: *Natural Law*, trans T. M. Knox, with an introduction by H. B. Acton, Philadelphia, University of Pennsylvania Press, 1975.

G. W. F. Hegel: *System of Ethical Life and First Philosophy of Spirit*, ed. and trans. H. S. Harris and T. M. Knox, Albany, State University of New York Press, 1979.

G. W. F. Hegel: *The Jena System, 1804–1805, Logic and Metaphysics*, translation ed. J. W. Burbidge and G. di Giovanni, Kingston and Montreal, McGill-Queen's University Press, 1986.

G. W. F. Hegel: *Hegel and the Human Spirit* (Second Philosophy of Spirit, 1805–1806), trans. L. Rauch, Detroit, Michigan, Wayne State University Press, 1983.

G. W. F. Hegel: *Science of Logic*, trans. A. V. Miller, London, England, Allen and Unwin, 1970.

G. W. F. Hegel: *Encyclopedia of the Philosophical Sciences in Outline* [Heidelberg, 1817] (and Critical Writings [Solger reviews]), ed. E. Behler, trans. S. H. Taubeneck, New York, Continuum, 1990.

G. W. F. Hegel: *Elements of the Philosophy of Right*, ed. Allen W. Wood, trans. H. B. Nisbet, Cambridge, England, The University Press, 1991.

G. W. F. Hegel: *The Encyclopedia Logic*, trans. T. F. Geraets, W. A. Suchting, and H. S. Harris, Indianapolis, Hackett, 1991. The references to *Enz.* in this book will be easily found here.

G. W. F. Hegel: *Philosophy of Nature*, trans. from *Encyclopaedia of the Philosophical Sciences* (1830) by A. V. Miller, Oxford, England, Clarendon Press, 1970.

G. W. F. Hegel: *Philosophy of Mind*, trans. from *Encyclopaedia of the Philosophical Sciences* by W. Wallace and A. V. Miller, Oxford, England, Clarendon Press, 1971.

G. W. F. Hegel: *The Philosophy of History*, trans. J. Sibree (1857), New York, Dover, 1956.

G. W. F. Hegel: *Lectures on the Philosophy of World History: Introduction*, trans. H. B. Nisbet with an introduction by D. Forbes, Cambridge, England, The University Press, 1975.

G. W. F. Hegel: *Introduction to the Philosophy of History*, trans. L. Rauch, Indianapolis, Hackett, 1988.

G. W. F. Hegel: *Aesthetics*, 2 vols., trans. T. M. Knox, Oxford, England, Clarendon Press, 1975.

G. W. F. Hegel: *Lectures on the Philosophy of Religion*, 3 vols., trans. E. B. Speirs and J. B. Sanderson, London, Kegan Paul, 1895; reprinted.

G. W. F. Hegel: *Lectures on the Philosophy of Religion*, 3 vols., trans. P. Hodgson et al., Berkeley, University of California Press, 1984–1987.

G. W. F. Hegel: *Lectures on the History of Philosophy*, trans. E. S. Haldane and F. H. Simson, 3 vols., London, Routledge and Kegan Paul, 1892; reprinted 1955.

G. W. F. Hegel: *Lectures on the History of Philosophy (The Lectures of 1825–1826)*, vol. 3, trans. R. F. Brown and J. M. Stewart, Berkeley, University of California Press, 1990.

3. Commentaries and Helpful Discussions

a) On Hegel's Intellectual Development

H. S. Harris: *Hegel's Development I: Toward the Sunlight* (1770–1801), Oxford, England, Clarendon Press, 1972.

H. S. Harris: *Hegel's Development* II: *Night Thoughts (Jena 1801–1806)*, Oxford, England, Clarendon Press, 1983.

Lawrence Dickey: *Hegel: Religion, Economics and the Politics of Spirit (1770–1807)*, Cambridge, England, The University Press, 1987.

G. Lukács: *The Young Hegel*, trans. R. Livingstone, London, Merlin; Cambridge, Mass, M.I.T. Press, 1976.

b) On the *Phenomenology*

H. S. Harris: *Hegel's Ladder*, 2 vols., Indianapolis, Hackett, forthcoming.

Terry Pinkard: *Hegel's Phenomenology: The Sociality of Reason*, Cambridge, England, The University Press, 1994.

Jean Hyppolite: *Genesis and Structure of the Phenomenology of Hegel*, trans. S. Cherniak and John Heckman, Evanston, Illinois, Northwestern University Press, 1974.

Joseph C. Flay: *Hegel's Quest for Certainty*, Albany, State University of New York Press, 1984.

Howard P. Kainz: *Hegel's Phenomenology*, 2 vols., Athens, Ohio University Press, 1983, 1988.

Alexandre Kojève: *Introduction à la phénoménologie*, Paris, Gallimard, 1979.

Quentin Lauer: *A Reading of Hegel's Phenomenology of Spirit*, New York, Fordham University Press, 1976; second edition, 1994.

Robert C. Solomon: *In the Spirit of Hegel: A Study of G. W. F. Hegel's "Phenomenology of Spirit"*, New York and Oxford, Oxford University Press, 1983.

Merold Westphal: *History and Truth in Hegel's Phenomenology*, Atlantic Highlands, New Jersey, Humanities Press, 1979; second edition (with new introduction) 1990.

c) On the System

John N. Findlay: *Hegel: A Reexamination*, London, Allen and Unwin, 1958.

Stephen Houlgate: *Reason, Truth and History*, London, Routledge, 1991.

Geoffrey R. G. Mure: *The Philosophy of Hegel*, Oxford, England, Clarendon Press, 1965.

Robert B. Pippin: *Hegel's Idealism*, Cambridge, England, The University Press, 1989.

Tom Rockmore: *Hegel*, Berkeley, University of California Press, 1994.

Charles Taylor: *Hegel*, Cambridge, England, The University Press, 1975.

Errol E. Harris: *An Interpretation of the Logic of Hegel*, Lanham, University Press of America, 1983.

Geoffrey R. G. Mure: *A Study of Hegel's Logic*, Oxford, England, Clarendon Press, 1950.

Shlomo Avineri: *Hegel's Theory of the Modern State*, Cambridge, England, The University Press, 1972.

Michael O. Hardimon: *Hegel's Social Philosophy*, Cambridge, England, The University Press, 1994.

Allen W. Wood: *Hegel's Ethical Thought*, Cambridge, England, The University Press, 1990.

George D. O'Brien: *Hegel on Reason and History*, Chicago, University of Chicago Press, 1975.

Emil L. Fackenheim: *The Religious Dimension in Hegel's Thought*, Bloomington, Indiana University Press, 1967.

Walter Jaeschke: *Reason in Religion*, trans. J. M. Stewart and P. C. Hodgson, Berkeley University of California Press, 1990.

Philip M. Merklinger: *Philosophy, Theology, and Hegel's Berlin Philosophy of Religion 1821–1827*, Albany, State University of New York Press, 1993.

Cyril O'Regan: *The Heterodox Hegel*, Albany, State University of New York Press, 1994.

Raymond K. Williamson: *Introduction to Hegel's Philosophy of Religion*, Albany, State University of New York Press, 1984.

James Yerkes: *The Christology of Hegel*, Missoula, Montana, Scholars Press, 1982; Albany, State University of New York Press, 1984.

Index